SERVING GRACE

Overseas Missionary Fellowship
1058 Avenue Road
Toronto, Ontario M5N 2C6

SERVING GRACE

Gifts without ' '

by
Michael Griffiths

MARC Europe
OMF Books

British Library Cataloguing in Publication Data

Griffiths, Michael, *1928-*
    Serving grace: gifts without inverted commas.
    1. Gifts, Spiritual
    I. Title
    234'.12   BT767.3

ISBN 0-947697-18-7 (MARC Europe)
        9971-972-40-9 (OMF Books)

MARC Europe is an integral part of World Vision, an international Christian humanitarian organisation. MARC's object is to assist Christian leaders with factual information, surveys, management skills, strategic planning and other tools for evangelism. MARC Europe also publishes and distributes related books on mission, church growth, management, spiritual maturity and other topics.

OMF Books is the publishing arm of Overseas Missionary Fellowship, formerly known as China Inland Mission. OMF's over 900 members work primarily in East Asia in evangelism and church planting, Bible teaching, and other ministries to strengthen the church.

Contents

Acknowledgements

My particular thanks are due to the Overseas Missionary Fellowship, who published the earlier book, *Cinderella's Betrothal Gifts;* also to my colleague Dr Max Turner for his article in the London Bible College theological journal, *Vox Evangelica*, XV (1985), and for innumerable discussions with him on various points. He should not be thought responsible for my ultimate conclusions!

Michael Griffiths, 1986

INTRODUCTION

Recently one of our students asked me, 'Will we be allowed to use "spiritual gifts" at Thursday's worship service, please?' I was at the same time amused and disappointed that he should use the phrase in that way, and so I replied, 'I don't see much point in holding the meeting at all unless we do!'

It is at once evident that the student was one of those today who use the words 'spiritual gifts' in a different and narrower sense than the Bible does. Yet these inverted commas seem to be in danger of becoming increasingly divisive among believing Christians.

This division is tragic, for what a sense of spiritual elation we enjoy when we know that the Lord has been pleased to use us, to empower us with his grace to speak or to serve. How properly euphoric we should all be when we realise afresh each time that in accordance with God's promises, the Holy Spirit has been our helper in the Christian service in which we have been engaged. We must not allow our differences of understanding to spoil in any way our experience of the grace of God in our lives, either congregationally or individually. It is a thrilling thing that our work and service in the churches are not capable of explanation by purely natural causes; we know the supernatural power of God at work among us.

Both Old and New Testaments speak of men being given *gifts* by the Spirit of God. This is so self-evident that it seems extraordinary that it should have become a source of disagreement between Bible-believing Christians. There is current in the churches today, however, a way of speaking about 'the gifts' that somehow puts them into inverted commas. 'In our church we believe in "the gifts".' The implication is that in other churches members somehow do not believe in 'the gifts' in quite the same emphatic way, or even perhaps that they mysteriously conduct their activities without the help of the Spirit of God at all.

It is now a common experience to hear someone speak in such a way of (ping, ping) *the gifts* (ping, ping) that you can almost physically feel those inverted commas flying through the air at you. It produces in some people such reaction that they rush to the opposite extreme.

Have the Gifts Ceased?

At the opposite end of the scale are people making the extraordinary assertion that the gifts described in the New Testament have long since ceased. The American branch of a certain well-known missionary society used to ask its applicants whether they had had any experience of 'char-ismatic gifts'. It seems that the correct answer anticipated was 'No'. The UK people were astonished, for a missionary who had no experience of charismatic gifts would be quite useless as a missionary, and almost certainly was not even converted yet. How could such a person be a Christian at all when Scripture says that the Lord gives gifts to each one according to his will (I Cor 12:11)? These apparently contra-dictory views seem to depend upon the inverted commas! No biblically educated Christian could deny that God gives gifts to men, that is, that he gives grace which is manifested in speaking and serving (I Peter 4:10-11) in ways which would not be possible unless those men and women were effectively empowered by God to speak and serve. How can one be a Christian without believing in the gifts of the Spirit? Who could function at all as a Christian without the exercise of such gifts? But the moment this universal Chris-tian conviction is differentiated as belief in 'the gifts', the emphasis and inflection of the words indicate that some-thing more than the straightforward meaning is intended.

Historically, the Christian Brethren, for example, have always believed in the exercise of spiritual gifts, especially as they met together around the Lord's table. They had no need to rediscover I Corinthians 14, for they always saw it as fundamental to their worship. They saw it also in contradistinction to priest-ridden one-man ministry. Even the most presbyter-ridden, one-man-band church would also affirm the necessity of that one man being given gifts by the Spirit for ministry, in addition to the gifts given to the other elders for their tasks. But neither the Christian Brethren nor the Free Church of Scotland, for example, have necessarily warmly embraced the 'charismatic movement', even though both groups believe sincerely in the gifts of the Spirit. Notice again those wretched inverted commas in 'charismatic movement', for properly understood the whole church is a charismatic movement, and every believer is biblically charismatic.

Evangelism and Church Planting Under-Emphasised

But there is another reason why we should be careful and thoughtful about much of the present debate. It tends to concentrate upon those gifts like prophecy, tongues, and healing about which Christians are not agreed among themselves. The Enemy thus uses the gifts of God, of all things, to confuse us and to deflect us from several more pressing issues. God's gifts are given both to edify the church and to take the gospel to the unbelieving world. Frankly, the unbelieving world is being neglected by the church: the percentage of full-time Christian workers set aside for evangelism and church planting, that is, long-term and frontline missionaries at home and overseas, is decreasing. We are supporting more workers at home, more musicians and 'establishment' people for large existing churches instead. We are so absorbed in arguing about our disagreements that we are seriously neglecting those gifts about which we have never disagreed. It is one of those distraction devices at which the Enemy is so adept.

Women's Ministry Under-Valued

Yet another area of concern is that the role of women in the church in relation to spiritual gifts is also being neglected. Some might feel that could be dismissed as yet another distraction ploy to take our eyes away from the main task; but the immobilising of more than 50% of Christians because they happen to be female is no peripheral matter. It could be said that for cultural reasons the women in our churches never have been fully or effectively mobilised. They are not being demobilised, but there is a great deal of understandable anger at the failure to recognise that in the New Covenant women are also priests and according to Joel's prophecy are to be equally endowed with spiritual gifts as their brothers. For this reason, after a general discussion of gifts, there is a whole chapter devoted to this important question. It is always difficult for Christians to disregard their cultural hangups, and 'Don't be conformed to this world.' (Rom 12:2) is one of the hardest commands to obey. Christians tend to try to make the Scriptures harmonise with their culture, rather than to reassess human traditions and attitudes in the light of Scripture. This is especially true where the role of women in society and the church is concerned.

The Scriptures Under-Used

It is always easier to find justification for some current practice in Scripture, rather than to arrive at that practice starting from the Bible itself. Infant baptism was always a case in point. However, the purpose of this book is to look afresh at the scriptural teaching about gifts. To consider the blessings which God in his grace has poured upon his church cannot be other than encouraging. Why should these inverted commas divide us from fellow believers? Who would dispute that many churches in the past have failed to recognise God's provision for effective ministry? It has been seen more as a product of theological education or of episcopal ordination, perhaps. But on the other hand, those who insist on using inverted commas seem to mean much more than a proper understanding of spiritual gifts. They associate spiritual gifts with chorus singing, raising one or both arms, jigging about with varying degrees of energy, and an excitement about allegedly direct words from the Lord, which rarely seems to be paralleled by an equal excitement and awe at the reading of (what we know without doubt is) the written Word of God. In some meetings there is far, far more singing of the words of men than the hearing of the Word of God. None of these outward cultural mores would seem in themselves to be essential to an authentic biblical understanding of gifts; indeed, some sincere Christians eschew them as forms of ostentation forbidden to Christian worship (Matt 6:5-8). We do not have to embrace a subculture as a package deal, with all its inverted commas, but rather we must examine that subculture carefully in the light of Scripture. This is what Paul advised the Thessalonians: 'Do not put out the Spirit's fire; do not treat prophecies wih contempt. *Test everything.* Hold on to the good. Avoid every kind of evil.' (I Thess 5:19-22) It is not unspiritual then, but properly biblical, to examine critically what goes on in the churches, to test everything, to keep what is good, and throw out what is bad.

The Danger of Putting Gifts Rather than the Giver in the Centre

Why is it important to test everything? Two personal experiences may help to illustrate this. In July 1974 I sat in the Swiss sunshine outside the Lausanne Congress building asking Festo Kivengere questions about how they handled misunderstandings during the East African Revival. He quoted William Nagenda as saying that Jesus Christ and him crucified must always be central. When any other doctrine or teaching moves into the central place, the church is in danger of following a false emphasis. At one time I was in danger of speaking more about the doctrine of the church than about the Lord whose Body it is. Yet today the centre of many churches is healing, or signs and wonders, or prophecies, or tongues, and these are the things that believers are excited about. This can be dangerous if the Lord is not glorified and central.

The Danger of Being Misled by Subjective Whimsies

The second experience is more recent. In September 1985 I was present at a church in Zagreb, Yugoslavia. A woman stood up to say that the Lord had spoken to her, and she wanted to share the word with the church. As she proceeded the church became very quiet, and my friend interpreting for me said, 'She says the Lord told her that more honour should be given to his mother Mary ... that the blood he shed on the cross had all come from her, so that it was her blood which was shed ... .' The expectation that the Lord will give direct messages to pass on to others faces this problem of subjectivism, leading people astray. The problem was dealt with most graciously. An elder rose, requested that she sit down, explained that the Lord Jesus Christ is worshipped as the divine Son of God in this church, and that while Mary was respected as his mother, she was also a sinful human being as we all are. Then he said, 'Now we will pray for our sister that she will come to a fuller understanding of biblical truth.' This error was so obvious that the church was not misled, but the danger of subjectivism is clear.

The Danger of Divisiveness

More than three hundred years ago the great Puritan John Owen wrote:

But now if there be that great diversity of gifts in the church, if so much difference in their administrations, how can it possibly be prevented but that differences and divisions will arise amongst them on whom they are bestowed ... it did so in this church of Corinth ... one boasted of this or that particular gift and ability, and would be continually in its exercise, to the exclusion and contempt of others, bestowed no less for the edification of the church than his own.[1]

In addition to the dangers of moving away from Christ as the centre, or accepting subjective whimsies in place of biblical certainties, there are the sad divisions within congregations or between churches. I hope that by removing the inverted commas we can bring one another closer to a common mind on this matter, remembering that God's purpose is that in the future we should all come to the unity of the faith (Eph 4:13). For it seems to me that sometimes these wretched little quotation marks have become divisive and sectarian. Can we not search the Scriptures together in such a way that we come closer to agreement about what the Lord has given us for the perfecting and upbuilding of the church? Even if we do not come to complete agreement with one another on every point, we shall at least understand better that those we disagree with are also endeavouring to be faithful to the Word of God. The inverted commas indicate differing interpretations of the same biblical material. In any given group there is often an accepted interpretation, but within another group the 'OK understanding' may be different.

The Importance of Definition

The same subjectivism determines that each of the gifts is defined, not according to Scriptures necessarily, but as determined by the human tradition of the subculture. The fact that we use a biblical word to describe an activity need not mean that it had the same meaning in the New Testament. We may say that 'word of wisdom', for example, means a kind of Christian clairvoyance. It might mean that, certainly, but we must be sure that it does not mean something quite different. So careful biblical study is very important to make certain each particular gift means what we think it means.

Relationship with Earlier Book

In writing on such a subject I am acutely aware of my own fallibility in understanding Scripture and fearful of a dogmatism based on my own ideas and experience. Such dogmatism would be no different from that about which I am expressing concern! My purpose must be always 'to Him be glory in the church and in Christ Jesus' (Eph 3:21), and this rewriting of an earlier book is a humble effort to maintain the unity of the Spirit through the bond of peace (Eph 4:3).

Some sections of this book must of necessity be the same as that of an earlier book entitled *Cinderella's Betrothal Gifts* in the UK and *Grace-Gifts* in the US. However, that was written some seven years ago and has been rewritten at the suggestion of MARC Europe in the light of more recent experience. I have had more direct experience of 'prophecy' and 'tongues' since the earlier book was written, and the debate over healing has continued. Much has been written that has been helpful, as well as much that tends to confuse.

With the passage of time and opportunity for reflection upon the arguments offered from all sides, I had hoped that Christians might have come more nearly to a common mind on this subject. But one seems to meet more and more unhappy Christians, who have felt obliged to leave churches of which they had been members for many years, or others who are hanging grimly on in situations with which they feel increasingly unhappy. Again and again one feels that, in spite of affirming a higher doctrine of the local church, the readiness with which people will divide from or split a local church fellowship reflects their not taking seriously enough those solemn words of the apostle Paul: 'Don't you know that you yourselves are God's temple, and that God's Spirit lives in you? If anyone destroys God's temple, God will destroy him; for God's temple is sacred, and you are that temple.' (I Cor 3:16-17) I write then with a deep sense of concern that Christians might know afresh what a joyful thing it is for brothers to dwell together in unity (Ps 133:1), even in mutual respect for our differences.

Footnote

[1] John Owen, *The Works of John Owen*, vol III (Banner of Truth: London, 1966), p 21.

CHAPTER 1

WHAT ARE SPIRITUAL GIFTS?

God the Holy Spirit is a Person, not a thing or an impersonal quantity. Perhaps because of words like 'pour' and 'fullness' in English this truth is often obscured, so that we may even think of receiving him as though some fluid were being poured into us. We must insist, when we think about our relationship with the Spirit, that we must think in terms of relationship with a *person*: an experience which must begin with an encounter, and which continues to deepen as we meet again and again and, indeed, walk together day by day.

Similarly the gifts of the Spirit are not to be visualised as being a number of gift-wrapped parcels, one or more of which we may have been given and more of which we might be given if we ask importunately enough. The very fact that they are called 'gifts' should warn against that. So what are they? Are they to be thought of as some additional chip, some kind of new programme, which may be added to our spiritual computer, so that we can then develop a new set of skills?

Let me define 'gifts' as abilities given to Christians through the grace of God for building up the churches, to glorify God in the world.

A Brief Word Study

There are at least five New Testament words translated 'gifts', and four of them derive from the root *do-* meaning 'give':

doron	used 19 times generally for men's gifts to one another and to God
dorea	used 11 times denoting primarily the gifts that God gives to men
dorema	used twice as in 'every good gift is from above' (James 1:17)
doma	used four times as in 'he gave gifts to men' (Eph 4:8)

The last two of these words end in the common suffix *-ma* indicating the result of an action. Thus the result of giving is a gift. The additional suffix *-ta* indicates a plural form.

Thus in Eph 4:8 the 'gifts' are people God gives for the equipment of the saints called *domata*. This word is made up of the stem to give — *do-* — with the ending *-ma* meaning 'the result of giving' that is a 'gift', and with the further addition of *-ta* indicating a plural number of such results of giving, i e 'gifts'.

The fifth and commonest word used for spiritual gifts is that from which we derive the currently popular word 'charismatic', and the rather inaccurate way in which it is frequently used (especially with inverted commas) requires us to look carefully at its biblical meaning and usage.

The meaning of *charisma* is not easy to define because we can learn almost nothing from material outside the New Testament; therefore the context is virtually our only guide.[1] It is thought that the apostle Paul may even have coined the word himself, for apart from I Peter 4:10, all the other 16 usages of the word are by Paul. The word *charisma* is derived directly from *charis* meaning 'grace', with the addition of the suffix *-ma* once again. A 'result of grace' then is a spiritual gift *charis-ma*. In the plural form it becomes *charisma-ta* meaning the many results of grace. This relationship is obscured because there is no direct connection between 'grace' and 'gift' in English, but the relationship is maintained in German where spiritual gifts are called *Gnadengaben* — that is, 'grace-gifts'.

This relationship in the original New Testament Greek

between grace and gifts is too obvious to be accidental as is clear from the following key passages about gifts:

> We have different gifts *(charismata)*, according to the grace *(charis)* given us.
>
> (Rom 12:6)

> Each one should use whatever gift *(charisma)* he has received to serve others, faithfully administering God's grace *(charis)* in its various forms.
>
> (I Peter 4:10)

> I always thank God for you because of his grace *(charis)* given you in Christ Jesus. For in him you have been enriched in every way — in all your speaking and in all your knowledge ... Therefore you do not lack any spiritual gift *(charisma)*.
>
> (I Cor 1:4-7)

When we think about spiritual gifts, we should always think of God's grace rather than gift-wrapped packets of power or abilities. Arnold Bittlinger writes, 'The origin of a *charisma* never lies in the person, but in God's grace which surrounds him. It is essential to bear in mind this origin whenever the gift is considered ... '[2] I have found it helpful to think of the illustration of white light falling upon a prism and being refracted into a spectrum of colours (an image which is also helpful in understanding overlap between gifts). So the grace of God shines upon the prism of the congregation and is then refracted into a spectrum of variegated 'grace-gifts'.

Gifts then are not to be thought of as personal attributes or acquisitions, but rather as outpourings of the grace of God upon the congregation, manifested as spiritual gifts exer-

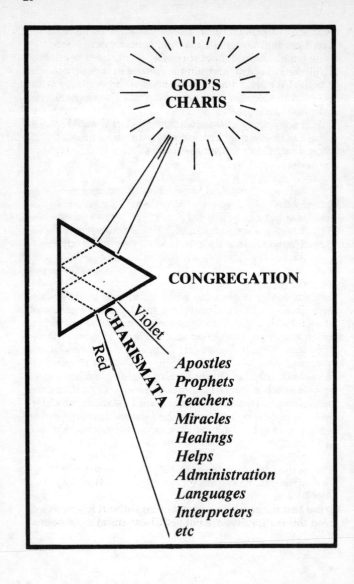

cised by individuals. John Goldingay defines *charisma* as 'God's grace finding particular and concrete actualisation';[3] while James Dunn defines it equally neatly as 'a particular manifestation of grace within the context of the community of faith'.[4] We have traditionally been so preoccupied with 'grace' in the form of God's common grace to all mankind, and particularly his saving grace to all believers, that we have tended to overlook this further usage of the word grace, which we might call *serving grace* or congregational grace. That is why this expression was chosen as the title of this book.

This concept throws much light upon other Scriptures. Thus Paul says, 'I worked harder than all of them, yet not I, but the *grace* of God that was with me.' (I Cor 15:10) We are told that 'with great power the apostles continued to testify to the resurrection of the Lord Jesus, and much *grace* was upon them all' (Acts 4:33) and that after hands were laid upon the Seven, already men full of the Spirit and of wisdom, Stephen 'a man full of God's *grace* and power, did great wonders and miraculous signs among the people' (Acts 6:8). Or 'You then, my son, be strong in the *grace* that is in Christ Jesus' (II Tim 2:1 in the context of teaching others). In all of these and many other places it cannot be saving grace that is referred to, but 'serving grace'.

In the writings of Paul, of the 16 references, several seem to be used in a much wider and more general sense than our present common usage of charismatic gifts more narrowly defined. It has the general sense of a favour bestowed, a gift of grace, that is a gift freely and graciously given, and thus by implication by God to men. Thus it is used:

of the free gift of salvation	Rom 5:15, 16; 6:23
of the gifts and calling of God	Rom 11:29
of the gift of continence	I Cor 7:7

Of the first usage we should note that without having been given this *charisma* we are not yet Christians at all. It seems wrong, therefore, that the word 'charismatic' should be used to describe only a limited group of Christians, when it must properly define every born again believer. On the other hand its use to describe celibacy, while not in any way a 'charismatic gift' in the usual sense, underlines our acceptance of singleness as being God's loving, gracious provision for some disciples. We should also notice that the word often translated 'spiritual gifts' in the opening verse of the classic passage (I Cor 12) is not actually *charismata* at all, but rather *pneumatikon*, and so in context may not mean 'spiritual gifts' at all. The genitive plural of the adjective *pneumatikon* may be neuter, meaning 'spiritual things' (as the same word does in I Cor 9:11; 14:1; 15:46) or masculine, meaning 'spiritual persons' (as the same word does in I Cor 2:25; 3:1; 14:37). It is probably masculine, meaning 'people who possess the Spirit'; or, as the context seems to demand, warning of the danger of being moved by false spirits and demons of dumb idols, so that we can translate I Cor 12:1 as 'Now about the inspired (persons), brothers, I do not want you to be ignorant.'

In What Sense Does an Individual Possess a Gift?

Perhaps the way in which we have tended to think of certain individuals in a congregation as possessing a particular spiritual gift as personal property, as it were, is a distorted emphasis. It is better to think of *charismata* as a variety of different ways in which the Lord graciously acts for the building up of the Church. Then the focus is upon the Giver and his goals, rather than upon the gift or the recipient who exercises the gift.

This is underlined by the way in which apostles, prophets, evangelists, and pastor/teachers may themselves be described as gifts *(domata)* of the ascended Christ to his victorious people (Eph 4:8). When we are thinking of the variety of edifying activities or functions being exercised by individuals *(charismata)*, it would be better to think of these as the pouring out of God's grace upon the congregation as a whole; to think of the manifestation of that grace being the variety of activities which we have come to describe as 'spiritual gifts'. The difference is more than a different emphasis; gifts are not so much possessed as exercised, under the operation of God's grace upon the congregation.

Some (notably Dunn)[5] think that Paul means that *charismata* are 'concrete actions, actual events, not ... latent possibilities and hidden talents'. In this view it is only particular occasions of teaching or specific utterances of prophecy which may be regarded as *charismata*. It is not so much 'talents on tap' as 'gifts given for a particular instance'. However, Hemphill[6] takes issue with this effectively, pointing out that Paul speaks of people being given gifts (I Cor 1:4; 4:7; 12:7; Rom 12:3; Eph 4:7) and of 'having' gifts (I Cor 8:1; 12:29-30; 13:1-3; 14:26; Rom 12:6) and gives practical instructions in I Cor 14 for utilising the gifts one has. Turner adds:

> Certainly he [Paul] expects the church to be characterised by a variety of gifts, and for these to be distributed in such a way that individual members of Christ are dependent on each other – but this must be made to suggest neither that each is a specialist with just one operation of the Spirit, nor, worse, that the Spirit's distribution of gifts is like some endless heavenly game of musical chairs with a different allocation of types of charismata each time the assembly meets.[7]

It is clear from the two references to Timothy's *charisma* in the Pastoral Epistles (I Tim 4:14 and II Tim 1:6) that Timothy has been given a gift which he is not to neglect, but to fan into flame. He has a responsibility to work at his gift to develop and cultivate it. It is in this sense that persons exercising the gifts of teaching or prophecy on a regular basis may be specifically described as teachers or prophets.

Thus laying on of hands (p 33 ff How Are Spiritual Gifts Received?) by the congregation or its leaders upon some-one being appointed as a teacher or pastor may be the means through which the appropriate gifts are mediated to the individual. But equally when someone moves out of some specific ministry in administration or children's evangelism, that gift may not have further opportunity of exercise and may be withdrawn. The emphasis must always be upon the sovereign gracious Giver so that the exerciser of the gift does not trust upon his possession of it, but humbly depends upon the grace of God, joined as a branch to the true vine with the supply of the Spirit flowing through to enable and make fruitful.

Footnotes

[1]Gerhard Kittel, *Theological Dictionary of the New Testament*, vol IX (Eerdmans: Grand Rapids, USA, 1972), p 403.

[2]Arnold Bittlinger, *Gifts and Graces: Commentary on I Corinthians 12-14* (Hodder & Stoughton: London, 1967), p 20.

[3]John Goldingay, 'The Church and the Gifts of the Spirit', *Grove Booklets on Ministry and Worship*, No 7 (1972), p 5.

[4]James Dunn, *Jesus and the Spirit* (SCM Press: London, 1975), p 207.

[5]*ibid*, p 209.

[6]K S Hemphill, *The Pauline Concept of Charisma* (Cambridge PhD Dissertation, 1976), p 78, footnote 92.

[7]Max Turner, 'Spiritual Gifts Then and Now', *Vox Evangelica*, vol XV (1985), p 31.

CHAPTER 2

WHY DO SPIRITUAL GIFTS OVERLAP?

It follows from what we have been saying about 'spiritual gifts' being manifestations of the 'manifold grace of God' (I Peter 4:10) that this grace can be experienced in many different ways. F F Bruce says concerning I Cor 12:11, the list is not intended to be exhaustive.[1] Thus in each of the lists the apostle is saying: When I use this word *charismata* I mean things like this and this and this etc etc. In responding to the question 'How many different gifts are there?' John Stott says, 'At least twenty are specified in the New Testament, and the living God who loves variety and is a generous giver may well bestow many, many more than that.'[2] For example, who would dispute that John Wesley or Francis Havergal, or some modern chorus writers had exercised grace-gifts in hymn writing, or that C S Lewis had a gift for writing books, although neither of these gifts is hinted at in the lists which we possess?

Because there are several lists which overlap partially with one another and because the same gift may be referred to under different names, or lumped together with others under some collective description, it has seemed helpful to bring this information together into one diagram.

In the first column we have taken the I Cor 12:28 list of eight gifts as normative because it sets gifts in some order of precedence as 'first, second, third . . . '.

In the second column, exactly the same sequence is found in the succeeding verses I Cor 12:29-32 listing only seven gifts, omitting both 'helps' and 'administrations' but adding 'interpreting'.

LISTS OF SPIRITUAL GIFTS COMPARED

I Cor 12:28	I Cor 12:29-32	I Cor 12:4-11	Rom 12:6-8	Eph 4:11	I Pet 4:10-11
'God has appointed'	'all are not...'	charismata energemata	charismata	domata	charisma
8 persons	7 persons	9 functions	7 functions	4/5 persons	2 functions
(first) APOSTLES	apostles			apostles	
(second) PROPHETS	prophets	prophecy	prophesying	prophets	
(third) TEACHERS	teachers	teaching of wisd/knowl	teaching	pastor/ teacher	'if anyone speaks...'
			encouraging		
				evangelist	
		faith			
worker of miracles	work miracles	miraculous powers			
gifts of healing	gifts of healing	gifts of healing			
able to help...			serving		'if anyone serves...'
			contributing show mercy		
gifts of admin			leadership (presiding)		
		discerning of spirits			
various kinds of tongues	speak in tongues	different tongues			
	interpret	interp			

I Cor 13:1-3	I Cor 14:26	GREEK	MEN	WOMEN
'If I have ...'	'each one has a ...'			
5 functions	5 contribs			
		apostoloi	Peter Andronicus	Junia
(prophecy)	apokalupsis (revelation)	prophetes	Silas Barsabbas	Anna
(all mystery) (all knowl)	(teaching)	didaskaloi	Agabus Lucius	Ti 2:4 Prisca
	(psalm)	parakaleo	Barnabas	
		evangelistes	Philip	Ph 4:3
(all faith)		pistis		He 11:35
(can move mountains)		dunameis	Stephen	
		charismata iamaton	Paul	
		antelempseis diakonia	The Seven	Dorcas
(give all)		ho metadidous ho eleon	Barnabas Onesiphor	Joanna Susanna
		kuberneseis proistamenoi	Stephanas	Phoebe I Tim 3:11
		diakriseis pneumaton	Peter Paul	
(tongues of men)	(tongue)	glossa	Paul	
	(interp)	hermeneia		

In the third column, the longest list I Cor 12:8-10, and sometimes therefore called 'The Nine Gifts of the Spirit', contains only five gifts found in I Cor 12:28.

In the fourth column, Romans 12:6-8, there is a list of seven gifts five of which do not correspond exactly with any in the Corinthian lists.

In the fifth column, Eph 4:11, the brief list of five (or more probably only four — see p 26) categories contain two new words, not found in Corinthians or Romans, and describing people, not functions, as *domata* and not *charismata*.

In the sixth column, Peter's simple division into verbal (presumably including apostles, prophets, pastors, teachers, and evangelists) and then non-verbal gifts (serving must include giving, showing mercy, leadership, administrations, and helps) seems almost too short for inclusion.

In the seventh column, the five spectacular gifts, which are nothing without the love described in I Cor 13, show their prominence in Corinth.

In the eighth column, the five contributions to public worship in I Cor 14:26 give further indication of the use of gifts in worship.

It would be possible to make many more comments about these lists, and most of them will be discussed under the relevant gift, e g 'the teaching of wisdom' and 'the teaching of knowledge' are regarded as part of the gift of 'teaching' (as explained on pp 63-68). There is manifestly considerable overlap between 'serving', 'giving', and 'showing mercy' in Romans, and the 'helps' of Corinthians, and a probable correspondence between those 'who lead' (or preside) in Romans and the 'administrations' of Corinthians. We therefore now need to discuss this overlap.

More Than One Gift for Each?

The whole argument of I Corinthians is that each Christian has a different gift, and that it is wrong to be jealous of the gifts of others. Paul is concerned to establish that each has a function to fulfil within the body.

> Now to each one the manifestation of the Spirit
> is given for the common good. To one there is
> given through the Spirit the message of wis-
> dom, to another the message of knowledge by
> means of the same Spirit, to another faith ... to
> another gifts of healing.
>
> (I Cor 12:7-9)

But this is not to be understood to mean that each person has only one gift — indeed this division of God's grace into separate, discrete packets is almost certainly wrong thinking, as we shall see.

It is obvious that some early Christian workers exercised several gifts — Paul and Barnabas are both listed among the 'prophets and teachers' in Antioch (Acts 13:1), yet shortly afterwards both are called 'apostles' (Acts 14:14). When Barnabas is first introduced to us (Acts 4:36-37) he is exercising the gift of 'giving' (Rom 12:8) while the use of a nickname 'Barnabas' (meaning son of encouragement) reminds us that he exemplifies that gift as well. He is also said to evangelise (Acts 13:32; 14:7), along with the apostle Paul. Paul on occasion manifested the gifts of healing and miracles, and appears to claim the gift of languages. Thus each of them appears to have exercised at least six gifts. Stephen was appointed to 'serve' (Acts 6:2) and possessed the gifts of faith (6:5) and miracles (6:8). Bearing in mind that Acts 7 contains 52 verses of the words of Stephen, together with his success in silencing the opposition of the Hellenistic Jews (who almost certainly included the uncon-verted Saul from Tarsus in Cilicia 6:10), we may conclude that he was verbally gifted as well as exercising non-verbal gifts.

Overlapping Between Gifts?

Even more confusing at first is the realisation that not only may one individual exercise several different functions, but that these biblical definitions themselves merge into one another and overlap. Our earliest illustration of a spectrum is helpful again, because now instead of reading as rigidly segregated gifts:

APOSTLE   PROPHET   TEACHER   SHEPHERD

they appear much more as a continuous spectrum:

APOSTLEPROPHETEACHERSHEPHERD

We find this overlap when the Antioch church leaders are described as 'prophets and teachers' without specifying which of the five named persons exercised which gift, and hinting that all five exercised both. Again, in Eph 4:11 the absence of the article before 'teachers' would seem to suggest that 'pastor/teachers' is one category rather than two. Could it be that the phrase 'apostles and prophets' in Eph 2:20 and 3:5 may conceal a further overlap between adjacent gifts? (See p 63).

Silas, included by Paul with Timothy and himself in I Thess 2:5 as 'apostles of Christ' is described as being 'a prophet' (Acts 15:32) when he said much to encourage and strengthen the brothers. So a prophet in fulfilling his ministry exercises the gift of encouragement. Prophecy is seen to overlap with other gifts in I Cor 14:31: 'For you can all prophesy in turn so that everyone may be instructed and encouraged.' This suggests that if we hear prophecy we are learning, and so being taught — also we are being encouraged. So prophecy overlaps two other gifts. 'All these activities, which shade too finely into one another for rigid distinctions to be profitable or even accurate, are of an advantage to the Christian assembly.'[3]

The spectrum illustration is again helpful. The colours may each be distinguished from one another as distinctively violet, blue or indigo, but each merges imperceptibly into the adjacent colours at the edges. The gifts of grace also appear like a spectrum in that each gift may be described as having its own nuance, its own distinctive purpose, and yet is bound to overlap considerably with its neighbouring gifts. Just as with light, grace is manifested in different wavelengths. Each word we use, like prophet, teacher, encourager, pastor, or evangelist, has its own distinctive shades of meaning, but both teaching and encouraging are aspects of the prophetic function. He is a poor evangelist who does no teaching. The effective church-founding apostle (see pp 46-47) must surely engage in evangelism, teaching, and encouraging as part of the apostolic task. We see this clearly in Acts 14 where the two apostles (v 4), give miraculous signs and wonders (vv 3, 8-10), evangelise (vv 7, 15, 21), strengthen and encourage (v 22). No one individual displays the whole spectrum of the gifts of God's manifold grace (though Paul must have come close to it), but one individual might exercise several related gifts.

This aspect of overlapping definitions can be very confusing, until we see them all as the varying wavelengths of grace, the consequences of the Lord blessing the congregation. If we concentrate on the Giver and his grace, rather than on the variety of gifts, we shall see the issues much more clearly, and I believe more biblically. This will also have relevance when we consider which of the gifts are manifested by women, and which perhaps are not. If prophecy and teaching overlap, then we must discover how a woman can prophesy without teaching! With all this in mind, let us consider how such gifts may be received.

Footnotes

[1] F F Bruce, '1 and 2 Corinthians', *New Century Bible* (Oliphants: Basingstoke, 1971), p 119.

[2] John Stott, *Baptism and Fullness* (IVP: Leicester, 1975), p 90.

[3] C K Barratt, *A Commentary on the First Epistle to the Corinthians* (Black: London, 1971), p 317.

CHAPTER 3

HOW ARE SPIRITUAL GIFTS RECEIVED?

When I made initial notes for this section, I immediately scribbled down words like 'seeking' and 'sovereignty', but when I started looking at the Bible itself, I was surprised to come up with different answers from those I had expected I would find on the basis of what I had been taught (exploding the myth that nobody was ever taught anything about spiritual gifts prior to the 1960's!). I found to my surprise that I had to qualify seriously the commonly accepted understanding of what 'seeking' or 'desiring' gifts really means, and that I had almost ignored what Scripture says about 'laying on of hands' in relation to spiritual gifts.

When God Sovereignly Bestows

A *free gift* is an unsolicited gift of grace bestowed by God himself. These gifts are particular ways in which God's gifts are realised for the congregation. We would all agree that grace-gifts are given by God (I Peter 4:10-11), by Christ (Eph 4:7-11), and by the Holy Spirit (I Cor 12:7-11). But there is an important question that is not often clearly verbalised, namely: *When* are spiritual gifts given to individual men of God? And to this there would be several answers.

Before We Are Born

God's sovereignty means that there are 'good works, which God prepared in advance for us to do' (Eph 2:10). The Lord had plans for Jeremiah before he was born, as is made clear when he says to Jeremiah: 'Before I formed you in the womb, I knew you, before you were born, I set you apart' (Jer 1:5). John the Baptist was 'filled with the Holy Spirit even from birth' (Lk 1:15), and Paul the apostle could speak of the Lord as one 'who set me apart from birth and called me by his grace' (Gal 1:15).

It is not that God is taken by surprise by our conversion and then has to make hasty decisions about what spiritual gifts he will endow us with. In his foreknowledge he has known all along that we were like the apostle Paul, 'a chosen instrument' (Acts 9:15). This means that we cannot drive a wedge between natural gifts and spiritual gifts — because God our Creator is not a different person from God our Redeemer, but one and the same God. It is not only that there is no reason why the Creator should not give natural aptitudes to his servants, which are subsequently sanctified and refined by his grace as spiritual gifts; but that there is every reason why the sovereign God should give to his servants in their mothers' wombs natural abilities, which when surrendered, tempered, and transfigured by God's grace may be effectively used for God's glory. The apostle Paul already showed marked gifts of initiative and leadership on that first of all missionary journeys to Damascus, even though his purpose then was to stamp out Christian groups rather than to plant new ones. John Stott expresses this well:

> In this case we must look for the peculiarities of the spiritual gift of teaching and encouragement in the heightening, the intensification, the 'Christianising' of a natural endowment already present, or at least latent. Thus a man may be a gifted teacher before his conversion,

and may after it be given the charisma of teaching to enable him to expound with insight, clarity and relevance.[1]

While we would agree that we cannot succeed in spiritual work merely by relying upon natural aptitudes — and we need God's grace if we are to be fruitful and effective — there is no reason to insist that spiritual gifts bear no relation at all to God-given natural aptitudes. It surely accords with spiritual common sense. If a man has a chaotically untidy mind by nature and cannot organise himself, let alone anybody else, it would seem a little unwise to entrust to him the steering of the congregation in anticipation that the Lord will give to him the gift of administration. God is sovereignly at work in our lives before we are born. We can see both our original genetic constitution and our subsequent spiritual endowments alike as both given by God and perfectly fitting together.

When God Endues Us with His Grace

In conversion the Holy Spirit comes to dwell in our hearts, and we become recipients of God's grace. While I can think of no scriptures that expressly speak of spiritual gifts being given at conversion, there are several which seem to imply that spiritual gifts have already been allotted to each Christian individual in the sovereignty of God:

> Think of yourself with sober judgement, in accordance with the measure of faith God has given you … . We have different gifts, according to the grace given us.
>
> (Rom 12:3:6)

> Now to each one the manifestation of the Spirit is given for the common good … . All these are the work of one and the same Spirit, and he

gives them to each man, just as he determines.

(I Cor 12:7:11)

But to each one of us grace has been given as Christ apportioned it.

(Eph 4:7)

At a time when there is strong emphasis on seeking certain gifts, it seems important to note the New Testament emphasis that every Christian possesses some spiritual gift already, sovereignly given by the Lord. Leon Morris expresses this clearly when he says:

> The local ministry could be exercised only because its members also possessed a *charisma*. The New Testament does not envisage any ministry as carried out apart from God's good gift.

> It is also to be borne in mind that all church members had a 'ministry' of some sort. 'The manifestation of the Spirit is given to every man' (I Cor 12:7) says Paul as he proceeds to the subject of ministering, and other references make it quite plain that this is no idle expression.[2]

When Hands Are Laid on Us by Church Leaders

A totally unexpected result of my Bible study was to discover that *charismata* required by the church might be bestowed by the 'laying on of hands'. The Giver is still God in his sovereignty, but he has chosen a channel, that is, the properly designated leaders of the local church. Let us look at two crucial New Testament passages:

> Do not neglect your gift, which was given you
> through a prophetic message when the body of
> elders laid their hands on you.
>
> (I Tim 4:14)

> For this reason I remind you to fan into flame
> the gift of God, which is in you through the
> laying on of my hands.
>
> (II Tim 1:6)

It is not clear whether both these verses refer to the same occasion, so that Paul together with the elders in Lystra laid hands on Timothy in the situation described in Acts 16:2-3. The similarity of the two expressions suggests that it is the same occasion, though not necessarily so. The relationship between the *charisma* and the laying on of hands is clear. I am not suggesting that God can automatically be manipulated by the performance of a ritual action; it is always his grace. But these verses clearly suggest that the normal and proper channel for the giving of spiritual gifts for exercise within the local church ought to be the laying on of hands by the leaders of that local church. J N D Kelly says:

> This action of laying, or rather pressing, hands
> on someone (the Hebrew verb is *samakh*), it
> should be noted, is entirely different from the
> 'placing' (Hebrew verb *sim* or *shith*) of the
> hands employed for blessings and healings,
> although the two are commonly confused and
> are rendered by the same Greek verb in both
> the Septuagint and the New Testament.[3]

This reminds us that the biblical background to this 'leaning on of hands' goes all the way back to the occasion when Moses pressed hands on Joshua (Num 27:18-23; Deut 34:9) having been commanded by God to do so. Thus Joshua was commissioned and was given some of Moses' authority even while Moses was still alive. Following Moses' death it is written that Joshua was 'filled with the spirit of wisdom because Moses had laid his hands on him'. When the Lord was speaking to the exhausted and discouraged Elijah on Mount Horeb, the Lord told him to return and then to 'anoint Elisha son of Shaphat from Abel Meholah to succeed you as prophet' (I Kings 19:16). Subsequently Elisha requested a double portion of Elijah's spirit, and he was certainly a worthy successor.

In the New Testament hands were laid upon the Seven when they were appointed. Though they were already men 'full of the Spirit and of wisdom' (Acts 6:3,6), hands were laid on them, and both Stephen and Philip subsequently manifested spiritual gifts in their ministries. The writer to the Hebrews assumes that the doctrine of laying on of hands is elementary teaching (Heb 6:2).

Leon Morris, contrasting early church ministry with the institutional ministry today, comments: 'Their ministry was exercised as the result of a special divine gift (charisma) and not of any human commissioning.'[4] It does, however, seem possible to understand the two Timothy references in such a way as to reconcile these two viewpoints. Decency and order in the church require that the local congregation seeks God's blessing and the bestowing of spiritual gifts required for service upon those whom it commissions as its leaders or sends out as missionaries. In the warm fellowship of the local church, its leaders lay hands on those who are being set apart for particular ministries, praying quite specifically that the sovereign Lord will be pleased to give them those *charismata* which they will need in order to fulfil their ministries — whether as church planting apostles, as pastor/teachers, or as those wise steersmen who will direct the future course of the church. These verses are an encouragement to believe that the Lord will be pleased to answer such prayer offered by the congregation in endowing Christian workers with his grace for service. It also may be more correct to see 'a gift' as part of the manifestation of the grace of God given to the whole congregation and less as a personally possessed piece of property.

Perhaps also the bestowing of *charismata* in answer to prayer may be seen as involved together with the laying on of hands. Thus Paul says: 'You help us by your prayers. Then many will give thanks on our behalf for the *charisma* granted us in answer to the prayers of many.' (II Cor 1:11)

When Do We Seek Gifts, or Is that a Misunderstanding?

When Solomon was invited to ask the Lord for whatever he wanted, he was commended because he asked for wisdom or a discerning heart (I Kings 3:9). It seems in character that God should ask us to make requests known to him, and what more appropriate than that we should ask for those grace-gifts that we need for the fulfilment of our ministry. In this general way, I have never hesitated to ask for all the help that I need so much. Without him, and the supply of his Spirit, we can do nothing. Having said that, I believe we need to study the Scriptures with great care at this point, if as we have seen the Lord has already endowed us with the grace that we need, and will add such graces as are required by fresh opportunities in answer to prayer and the appointment of the congregation. The whole argument of I Cor:12 seems to be that we should accept that role, whether mouth or eye, arm or leg, which the Lord had already sovereignly determined, and not to wish that we might take on also the roles and functions of others (vv 14-30).

Until I did this study I had always assumed for many years that the Lord placed upon us the responsibility to *seek* for spiritual gifts, and that if we had an opportunity to serve we should then ask for the gift appropriate to that ministry. Many of my contemporaries as students back in the early fifties prayed for the gift of teaching. We need to look at Scripture much more carefully, and especially those three verses that immediately spring to mind in this matter of 'seeking' for gifts:

But eagerly desire *(zeloute)* the greater gifts *(charismata)*

(I Cor 12:31)

eagerly desire *(zeloute)* spiritual gifts *(pneumatika)* especially that you prophesy

(I Cor 14:1)

Therefore, my brothers, be eager *(zeloute)* to prophesy.

(I Cor 14:39)

The traditional understanding of 12:31 is that we should seek gifts. But there would seem to be several questions and qualifications to be made about this issue.

First, is this addressed to Christian individuals each to seek for themselves those gifts they feel that they need, or is it addressed to the whole congregational body, urging them to seek such gifts as they need for their proper corporate functioning together? That is, though one individual will possess only some gifts, the Church needs them all, and it is perfectly proper, therefore, for the *Church* to seek them.

Second, there seems to be a contradiction in this verse as traditionally understood, because the members of the body have been urged to accept that they have different gifts and that they should not therefore be jealous of those who have been sovereignly given other gifts: the ear is to accept that it is not an eye, and the foot that it is not a hand. If Paul has admonished them to be content with the gifts that God has given to them, it seems quite extraordinary that he then ignores his own argument and urges them to desire the greatest gifts![5] If he has told them not to waste time wishing they were somebody else with different gifts, why now does he tell feet to desire eagerly to become hands?

Third, it seems possible, therefore, to read *zeloute* not as a command, an imperative: 'Seek gifts!', but as an indicative, a statement about them: 'You eagerly desire the greater gifts (which you ought *not* to be doing). And now I will show you the most excellent way.' This view is much strengthened because in describing love, the first negative thing Paul says about love is that it is 'not jealous' *(zeloi)* (I Cor 13:4). Moreover, much earlier in the epistle Paul says that the Corinthians are still childish and carnal because there 'is jealousy *(zelos)* and strife among you' (I Cor 3:3). This would then mean that Paul tells them *not* to be jealous of one another's gifts, but to seek the more excellent way: love.[6]

Fourth, I Cor 14:1 does not use the word *charismata* but *pneumatika*, that is, 'spiritual things', so in any event is not a command to seek gifts, so much as that which is spiritual — 'the way of love' (same verse).

Fifth, how should we then translate the verb *zeloo*, which occurs in all three of these verses? It has been translated in English as 'seek', 'desire', or 'covet'; and this has caused all the confusion, because most of us therefore assumed that we should actively seek the greater gifts — those described as 'First of all apostles, second prophets, third teachers . . .'.

But have we been translating the word correctly?

Zeloute is the root from which both 'zealous' and 'jealous' derive. It is used generally of being zealous for God and especially of Jews' hostile attitude to the Romans and to Christian preaching. Kittel[7] suggests that it means 'a human emotion which leads to action ... to strive after something, the consistent and zealous orientation of action to a moral ideal'. The use of the same root in other passages seems relevant here: 'zealous for good deeds' (Titus 2:14) and 'if you prove zealous for what is good' (I Peter 3:13). We would not regard this as meaning a pious waiting and praying for good deeds. We would urge them to go out and do them, practise them!

This suggests that being zealous for charismata *means enthusiastic hard work to develop and cultivate spiritual gifts already sovereignly given by God to us, rather than praying for a gift one does not yet have, all done up in a neat package.*

This understanding seems to be born out by what Paul tells Timothy in relation to the *charisma* which he has been given (I Tim 4:7-17): 'devote yourself ... Do not neglect your gift ... be diligent in these matters; give yourself wholly to them, so that everyone will see your progress ... Persevere in them ... .' The same stress on responsibility to work at cultivating your gift is found also in II Tim 1:6: 'I remind you to fan into flame the gift of God ... .' Both of these passages about a *charisma* given through the laying on of hands stress the responsibility to take pains and give effort to the development and cultivation of the gift. It seems to me that this is the same thing that Paul says to the Corinthians when he tells them to be zealous for spiritual gifts: not meaning the seeking of gifts that we do not have, but rather working to develop the gifts we have already been given by God.

Conclusion

Gifts are the sovereign gift of God, often decided before birth, but manifest subsequent to conversion, when the indwelling Spirit sanctifies God-given natural aptitudes through his grace. Gifts for particular ministries may be mediated to individuals through the laying on of hands before the congregation, endowing them with special gifts as required by the ministry to which the church is appointing them.

While the Lord may be pleased to respond to our praying for grace, and our requests for gifts that we do not possess, our chief responsibility is to cultivate and develop those gifts which he has given to us already in his sovereignty.

Footnotes

[1] See John Stott, *Baptism and Fullness* (IVP: Leicester, 1975), pp 90-94.

[2]Leon Morris, *Ministers of God* (IVP: Leicester, 1964), p 62.

[3]J N D Kelly, *The Pastoral Epistles, Black's New Testament Commentaries* (Black: London, 1976), p 106-107.

[4]Morris, *op cit*, p 62.

[5]See Gerhard Iber, quoted by Bittlinger, *op cit*, p 73.

[6]Wayne A Grudem, in *The Gift of Prophecy in First Corinthians* (University Press of America: Maryland, 1982), p 56, footnote 111, has criticised this view. He says that 'the hortatory character of the entire passage and the parallel in 14:1 require that *zeloute* here be an imperative and not an indicative'. The same view is held by Orr and Walther, 'I Corinthians', *Anchor Bible* (Doubleday: New York, 1976). However, it seems to me that the argument against Paul's contradicting himself is a stronger one.

[7]Gerhard Kittel, *Theological Dictionary of the New Testament*, vol II (Eerdmans: Grand Rapids, USA), p 886ff.

CHAPTER 4

HOW MAY SPIRITUAL GIFTS BE DEFINED?

It is, unfortunately, common for people to start from contemporary experience, and then to identify this with a biblical phrase. We must first try to discover how these words were used in the Bible, although we must also recognise that when a word only occurs once or twice, it is impossible to be definite and therefore foolish to be dogmatic. In some instances there is a wealth of biblical material, and there are several recent studies – Aune and Grudem on prophecy, Turner and Hemphill on *charismata* – which were not available when I wrote *Betrothal Gifts* in Singapore in the mid-seventies.[1]

For example, 'prophecy' in contemporary, secular English almost always means prediction about the future. Thus Turner starts by saying: 'We can base no conclusions on the results of study of word-formation or etymology – words change their meanings with time, and we are only interested in synchronic analysis: what the words meant in Paul's day.'[2] Let us then take the gifts in the order in which they appear in the I Corinthian 12:28 list, but inserting other verbal gifts after the three placed in sequence.

Apostles

The gift of an apostle is described as 'first' and in the lists of gifts is mentioned specifically three times, always as a personal office and not as an aptitude. Confusion arises because some insist that an apostle can only be defined in terms of this passage:

> one of the men who have been with us the whole time the Lord Jesus went in and out among us, beginning from John's baptism to the time when Jesus was taken up from us. For one of these must become a witness with us of his resurrection.
>
> (Acts 1:21-22)

Clearly, defined in these terms, an apostle had to have been a member of the band of Jesus's disciples who had witnessed all three years of his ministry and lifestyle, including especially the Resurrection. In this sense then — of the Twelve — they were unique and could not have any successors. Their unique authority is to be found in Scripture alone. (This position is essential to evangelical Anglicans faced with those who claim that apostolic authority is now vested in the apostolic succession of bishops. It has been less of a problem to non-Anglicans until more recently.)

This understanding of where apostolic authority now lies is crucial. Those of us who are willing to accept the continuing existence of 'apostles' in some lesser sense should never allow that to diminish the authority and sufficiency of Holy Scripture in any way, as the Lord's revelation through Moses and the prophets, and supremely in his Son Jesus Christ, and his apostles.

Lesser and Secondary Senses

There are other ways, however, in which some would recognise that apostles may still be given by God to his people, in a lesser sense.

The Pioneer church planting missionary Scripture itself does speak of some who were not members of the Twelve as apostles, including Paul and his several associates: Barnabas (Acts 14:14), Silas and Timothy (I Thess 2:6), Andronicus and Junia (Rom 16:7 where Junia is probably feminine – see p 108), Epaphroditus 'your apostle' (Phil 2:25), and the apostles of the churches (II Cor 8:23). The fact is that they are called 'apostles' in Greek, but then translated 'messengers' and the like, precisely in order to avoid confusion with the Twelve apostles. We realise therefore that the Bible uses the word in a much more general sense of someone sent on a mission by a church. Thus Paul uses the verb *apostello* three times: of preachers being 'sent' (Rom 10:15); of being 'sent' to preach the gospel (I Cor 1:17), and of Paul's 'sending' of his own deputies (II Cor 12:17).

Goldingay points out that *apostolos* is etymologically equivalent to 'missionary' and says that 'Apostles are perhaps the pioneer missionary evangelists through whom Christian communities are founded.'[3] This meaning is supported by I Cor 9:2 where Paul says to the church, 'Even though I may not be an apostle to others, surely I am to you', that is, as the missionary founder of the Corinthian congregation. This can be parelleled by other expressions, e g, 'I planted . . . by the grace God has given me, I laid a foundation as an expert builder' (I Cor 3:10) and 'you do not have many fathers . . . I became your father' (I Cor 4:15).

The pioneer missionary going to a new tribe discovers that the people have no Bible in their own language. The missionary is their only source of apostolic doctrine, so that even in this limited sense, he carries apostolic authority. It does not seem biblically that it is necessary to deny the continuing existence of apostles in this secondary sense of pioneer church planting missionaries, e g 'George Hunter: Apostle to Turkestan'.

One of the great needs of missions today is people endowed with this essential *charisma*. It is the 'first' of the gifts, and the planting of new congregations is the supreme need still in many parts of the world. In addition to sending out those who will work in medicine, translation, literature, or relief, we need to recognise afresh the primacy of this apostolic gift – that of the pioneer church planter.

The peripatetic Bible teacher Having listened to a very win-some presentation of this possibility from a leader in the House Church movement, I find myself much less hostile and more sympathetic to the concept. If pastor/teachers minister in the local congregation, then some term must be found to describe the gifted teacher who ministers in *many* churches. To use the word 'apostle' in this sense would not seem illegitimate in itself, unless it is accompanied also by arrogant authoritarianism. One also might question the wisdom of actually being called 'apostle' in view of possible misunderstandings.

Dangers to Avoid

I do find some danger in a recent book which urged Christians to watch and pray for apostles to be raised up and to recognise and submit to them as they appear. This seems quite different from the New Testament, where apostles bring new congregations into existence. We should beware of self-styled apostles who wish to put themselves into authority over us, and especially of status seekers who split churches in order to grasp at a prominence denied them by society and responsible church discipline.

In view of the modern distrust of authority in general, it is good to find today a fresh recognition of proper authority in the local church. In the past there were too many spiritual freelances floating round without membership in or discipline from any congregation of saints. 'Obey your leaders', we read in Hebrews 13:17. However, it is important we should recognise the limits attached to the leaders in the New Testament. It seems foolish that Protestants who have rejected the authority of the Pope in Rome should exchange him for an inferior local pope demanding absolute obedience and submission to his fallible interpretations of Scripture or apprehensions of the will of God for others.

The Bible limits the authority of leaders. The apostles

refused to obey the commands of Israel's legitimate religious leaders (Acts 4:19-20). Paul withstood the apostles
to the face when he knew them to be wrong (Gal 2:11).
Scripture knows nothing of infallible religious leaders (I Cor
8:2; 13:9). Even authoritative preaching from the pulpit is
not beyond Spirit-guided criticism (I Cor 14:29; I Thess
5:21). Prophesying and preaching are mixed phenomena:
even Spirit-filled utterance may be mixed with fleshly elation, half-truth and even error; therefore, both must be
tested and weighed. It is a Christian duty to exercise our
critical faculties, albeit with much courtesy and charity. We
do no Christian teacher a service by regarding his teaching
as infallible.

Even though Paul reminds the Corinthians of his apostolic authority, he then goes on to appeal to their independent judgement in I Cor 10:15: 'I speak to sensible people;
judge for yourselves what I say.' Though Paul never calls
Timothy or anyone else his 'disciple', Timothy was certainly his protégé and 'child in the faith', yet even to him
Paul says, 'Reflect on what I am saying, for the Lord will
give you insight into all this.' (II Tim 2:7) The Christian,
therefore, is to use his own judgement, and not merely to
accept what his spiritual father may say.

The most compelling passage of all is Romans 14, where
Paul says, 'Each one should be fully convinced in his own
mind.' (v 5) Even with the full apostolic authority that Paul
possessed, he did not tell the Romans what they were to
believe about abstaining from food or observing days, but
urged them to follow their own conscience. The believer is
finally answerable only to his One Lord, his own master (v
4) because 'each of us will give an account of himself to
God.' (v 12) The Christian is not to abdicate his direct
responsibility to God alone — the right of private judgement was a precious achievement of the Reformation ob-
tained at the cost of many martyrs' lives. It should not be
usurped by any human leader in the name of authority or
shepherding.

Peter writes to elders about the style of Christian leadership: *'not lording it* over those entrusted to you, but being examples to the flock' (I Peter 5:3), deliberately recalling the instructions of the Lord Jesus contrasting Christian leadership with that of secular Gentile leadership: 'the rulers of the Gentiles *lord it over* them ... *not so with you'* (Matt 20:25). Jesus then contrasts with Jewish religious leadership with its love of impressive highsounding titles:

> But you are not to be called 'Rabbi', for you have only one Master and you are all brothers. And do not call anyone on earth 'father', for you have one Father, and he is in heaven. Nor are you to be called 'teacher', [a rare word which is used for professor in modern Greek] for you have one Teacher, the Christ.
>
> (Matt 23:8-10)

Paul also uses the same word as Peter when he says, 'Not that we lord it over your faith, but we work with you' (II Cor 1:24); while Luke amusingly uses the word for the demon-possessed lunatic who 'overpowers' the seven sons of Sceva (Acts 19:16). The Christian leader who 'lords it over' others is behaving like a lunatic, and far, far worse, disobeying the clear teaching of the Lord and the apostles about Christian leadership style — through humble service and good example.

Personally, I have no problems about the use of the word 'apostle' today, provided it is clear that Scripture has higher authority, and as long as apostles today are as humble as those of the New Testament, recognising the believer's right to independent judgement, answerable to his own Master alone.

Prophets

Prophecy is the most commonly referred to of all the gifts. It comes in no less than seven lists, against the single reference each to 'pastors' and 'evangelists'. Peter declares it to be a universal mark of the new age:

> I will pour out my Spirit on all people.
> Your sons and daughters will prophesy,
>   your young men will see visions,
>   your old men will dream dreams.
> Even on my servants, both men and women,
>   I will pour out my Spirit in those days,
>   and they will prophesy.

(Acts 2:17-18)

And Peter is saying that Joel's prophecy is now fulfilled. Notice that Peter has added the words 'and they will prophesy' not found in Joel, thus implying that the gift will be common among Christians, fulfilling the hopes of the Old Testament that 'all God's people should prophesy' (Num 11:29).[4] If it is a sign of the new age, we should hesitate before accepting the view that this gift no longer exists.

Do All Prophesy or Only Some?

There is an underlying problem here in that while some are actually called prophets, many others may prophesy on occasion. F F Bruce commenting upon 1 Cor 14:31 says that:

> The ability to prophesy, at least on occasion, is open to most, indeed to all, members of the church, although only a few may exercise it at any one meeting, speaking one by one, so that all may learn, and all be encouraged. In 11:4f, prophesying appears to be as common an exercise as praying and that on the part of men and women alike.[5]

The *New Bible Dictionary* even says, 'Every Christian is potentially a prophet.'[6] Earle Ellis explains helpfully:

> In several passages in Acts, the phenomenon of
> prophecy is ascribed to Christian disciples gen-
> erally ... alongside these texts is the equally
> significant fact that Luke restricts the term or
> title *prophetes,* as it is used of his contempora-
> ries, to a select number of 'leading men' (cf Acts
> 15:22) who exercise considerable influence in
> the Christian community.

He then goes on to cite the group from Jerusalem visiting
Antioch, which included Agabus (Acts 11:27ff), a group
resident in Antioch, including Paul (Acts 13:1) and the two
prophets who accompanied the Jerusalem decree to Antioch, Judas Barsabbas and Silas (Acts 15:22-23). As we shall
see later, these particular men are not the only prophets in
Acts, or the only individuals named as prophesying in the
New Testament (p 108).

Thus there does seem to be a difference between the
prophesying in which all Christians may properly engage
one by one, and those who are specifically given the title of
'prophets'. At the same time, Paul asks 'Are all prophets?'
(I Cor 12:29) in a form expecting a negative answer, that is,
'All are not prophets, are they?' and yet seems to encourage
them to value prophecy highly, much more than languages
(I Cor 14). But we have seen that a letter addressed to a
congregation may encourage them to cultivate the gifts of
prophecy they already have, rather than being an injunction to every believer to seek an identical gift to others.

How Authentic Is New Testament Prophecy Compared with the Old?

John Stott is understandably concerned lest present day
phenomena are identified with canonical Old Testament
prophecy:

> The biblical understanding, dating back to Old

Testament days, is that a prophet was an organ
of divine revelation, to whom the Word of the
Lord came, and who therefore spoke the very
words of God (e g Ex. 4:12; 7:1-2; Jer. 1:4-9;
23:16, 18, 22, 28). In this meaning of the term,
which is the essential biblical meaning, I think
we must say that there are no more prophets,
for God's self-revelation was completed in
Christ and in the apostolic witness to Christ,
and the canon of Scripture has long since been
closed.[8]

He rightly then wants us to be cautious about 'other and
lesser senses', and for himself concludes that there are
neither apostles nor prophets today. This is the simplest
and most straightforward solution, but it leaves in limbo
many sincere Bible believers, who experience something
they choose to call prophecy in their meetings.

As with apostleship, we may readily concede the possibility that we are still able to speak of prophecy, but in a
lesser sense, and with a much weaker signal, than we have
received from the canonical Prophets. Grudem's full treat-
ment of this subject and other recent discussion is helpfully
summarised by Turner.[9]

It would be easy to assume that New Testament prophets
were the same as Old Testament prophets. However, Grudem suggests that:

those who are viewed as divinely authoritative
messengers in the New Testament are most
often called not 'prophets' but 'apostles' ... if
the New Testament apostles are frequently
seen as the counterparts to the Old Testament
prophets, then New Testament prophets might
often be something quite different.[10]

This seems to be expressed directly in II Peter 3:2, and Eph
2:20 can be read in the original to mean 'the apostles who

are also prophets'.

It is suggested that prophets in the New Testament are much less convincing and authoritative sources of revelation. The arguments are as follows:

(1) Paul subordinates prophets to his own authority (I Cor 14:37-38).

(2) Prophecy is still only partial misty knowledge (I Cor 13:9).

(3) Prophecy can be so unconvincing, it can be despised (I Thess 5:19ff).

(4) Prophecy is not to be automatically accepted as true, but has to be sifted, and weighed, being such a mixed phenomenon (I Cor 14:29 and I Thess 5:20-21).

(5) Paul never reinforces his statements by claiming to be a prophet, but rather by reminding them that he is an apostle.

(6) In the Old Testament instructions are given for dealing with false prophets (e g Jeremiah 23:16-40; 28:9), but in the New Testament they are told to assess the content of prophecies, and there is no suggestion that if someone's words were weighed and found wanting that he or she would then be judged a false prophet. This certainly removes the pressure when someone does seem to be saying something improper.

(7) It is accepted that the words of some prophecies might never be heard by the congregation, and lost, when one sits down (I Cor 14:30).

David Atkinson in his most helpful monograph is very clear:

> What must be recognised in today's church, however, is that claims to prophecy are not, and should not be treated as claims parallel to

the voice of Amos or Ezekiel, or the author of
Revelation. They are parallel, rather, to the
much less authoritative, but none the less valid
functions such as were exercised by the church
prophets of Corinth.[11]

Turner sums up this view as follows:

> The presupposition is that any one New Testa-
> ment prophetic oracle is expected to be mixed
> in quality, and the wheat must be separated
> from the chaff. The prophet may genuinely
> have received something from God (albeit often
> indistinctly), but the 'vision' is partial, limited
> in perspective, and prone to wrong interpreta-
> tion by the prophet, even as he declares it (I Cor
> 13:12).[12]

The contrast may be overdrawn, for Paul seems to accept
that even apostles only 'know in part, and prophesy in
part' (I Cor 13:9), yet it seems clear that New Testament
prophecy does not carry the authority of canonical prophecy in the Old Testament or the book of Revelation.

To What Extent Is New Testament Prophecy Predictive?

We meet a problem here in that the English word 'prophecy' implies foretelling the future, and it is difficult to shake
off that nuance of the word. In Acts there are only three
examples of predictive prophecy: in Acts 11:28 Agabus'
prediction of famine to spread over the Roman world, in
Acts 21:10-11 Agabus' prediction of Paul's arrest and captiv-
ity, and in Acts 28:25-28, perhaps, where Paul says Isa 6:9-
10 is now fulfilled.

The Corinthian believers were told that they could all
prophesy one by one; and if all their prophecies at every
meeting were all prediction of future events, it would have

become somewhat overwhelming! It would then appear that much more would have been related to the immediate situation. Indeed, Old Testament prophecy, while containing also predictive passages, is much more social commentary on the existing scene.

Three descriptions of prophecy given in the New Testament (they cannot be regarded strictly as definitions) significantly make no mention of predictive elements; so perhaps we are correct in thinking this was a relatively rare and minimal element in congregational prophecy.

> Judas and Silas, who themselves were prophets, said much to encourage and strengthen the brothers.
>
> (Acts 15:32)

> But everyone who prophesies speaks to men for their strengthening, encouragement and comfort.
>
> (I Cor 14:3)

> For you can all prophesy in turn so that everyone may be instructed and encouraged.
>
> (I Cor 14:31)

Significantly, the common element to these three descriptions is encouragement, and there is no suggestion at all of anything predictive. (See page 70-71 on the gift of encouragement.)

From the example of Agabus, and perhaps the Lord's revelations to Paul in dreams and visions (e g Acts 18:9-10; 23:11; and 27:23-26), the prophecies seem to have been addressed to particular individuals in particular situations, and without permanent significance or lasting application in other situations.

How Should We Define Prophecy?

Here are several definitions:

It is a specific form of divination that consists of intelligible verbal messages believed to originate with God and communicated through inspired human intermediaries.[13]

> Prophecy is the reception and subsequent communication of spontaneously, divinely given apokalypsis.[14]

> Prophecy is the gift by which God speaks through a person a message to an individual or a whole Christian community. It is God making use of someone to tell men what He thinks about the present situation or what his intention is for the future, what he thinks that they should know or be mindful of right now. Prophecy is not necessarily for prediction of the future (although this frequently happens).[15]

> It is the gift by which God keeps his church up-to-date, able to understand and live in the changing world.[16]

> It was the direct word from God for the situation on hand, through the mouth of one of his people (and on occasion, this could apparently be any Christian, including those not reckoned to be 'prophets').[17]

There is however a biblical passage which perhaps needs to be looked at much more carefully, for while it describes the activity of Old Testament canonical prophets, it throws much light on what was involved.

> The prophets, who spoke of the grace that was to come to you, searched intently and with the

greatest care, trying to find out the time and circumstances to which the Spirit of Christ in them was pointing when he predicted the sufferings of Christ and the glories that would follow.

(I Peter 1:10-11)

In other words, the prophets were diligent Bible students, comparing scripture with scripture. They did not merely speak *ex vacuo* words that popped into their minds, but scrutinised intently and searched extensively (*exezetesan kai exeraunesan* – beautiful and polished Greek alliteration). The first word, as in Deut 4:29 'if you seek the Lord your God', speaks of an intensive moral search. The second word implies searching with some difficulty for something that is hidden, as Prov 2:4, 'Look for it as for silver and search for it as for hidden treasure'. It was both intensive scrutiny and extensive searching over an extensive area – in this case the whole Scripture. The prophet Daniel (12:6-8) tells us that he was studying Jeremiah. When we read Malachi 3:6 we find echoes both of Lam 3:22-23 and Zech 1:3. Yes, Malachi is prophesying in a new situation, but he sees the relevance of what the Lord has already said in earlier situations through earlier prophets. (If Calvin is correct in seeing Malachi as a pseudonym for Ezra, we know what a diligent student of scripture he was, Ezek 7:10). Two New Testament examples would be Zechariah (Luke 1:67ff) of whom it is said 'Zechariah was filled with the Holy Spirit and prophesied . . . .' He quotes extensively from the Psalms (which he would have sung daily in the temple) and the prophets, including Malachi. Or again, Simeon, who in the four short verses of the *Nunc Dimittis* quotes no less than five different chapters of Isaiah (Luke 2:29-32). Or finally think of the apostle John on Patmos (which prophets would you study in exile?) studying the prophets of the exile, Daniel and Ezekiel, and steeped in their language and imagery (Rev 1:9ff).[18]

This is an important understanding. Prophets are diligent students of the scriptures, conditioned by the Word of God, not mere mouthpieces, sharing their ignorance with us. Ellis makes an interesting suggestion:

> It is probable that not only the miracle-working context but also the manner of Jesus' exposition of Scripture in the synagogue contributed to the conviction he was a prophet. And it could do so because such exposition was regarded as the proper activity of a prophet.[19]

Doubts and Concerns about Contemporary 'Prophecy'

Writing in 1981, a lecturer of St John's College explained that most weeks there would be opportunity for the exercise of 'charisms' in college chapel. He said that on a fair number of occasions people brought tongues, followed by interpretation, prophecies or 'pictures', and made this comment after several years' experience:

> We had received a number of prophecies etc in college chapel, but never with the degree of freedom that people who were in the heart of the renewal movement longed for. Further, these messages mostly seemed to reflect only too clearly the background and inner personal needs of the messengers, and the number that (in my view) spoke with clear authenticity and challenge was very small.[20]

Frankly, my own experience in another college has been equally disappointing. Many 'prophecies' have been largely hortatory, and people have called them 'innocuous', which would seem entirely inappropriate for anything that purports to come from the Lord — whatever else Old Testament prophets might have been, 'innocuous' they certainly were not! Once or twice in the past five years there have been words that seemed to put their finger on our failures. When we were putting up a new building, we were reminded that building a spiritual house of living stones was much more important, and I found that genuine. Twenty or thirty years earlier the same thing might have been said during chapel ministry, but not cast in the form of prophecy. Most of the time there was nothing that might be called anti-scriptural, though on one occasion something was said that seemed to me and others to be quite wrong.

At such times one is glad that we are expected to weigh what has been said, and that Scripture itself indicates that New Testament prophecy is a 'mixed' phenomenon. We all have the experience, when preaching, of saying something more clearly or more simply than we had intended beforehand. There is always this element that is supernatural, and which we would ascribe to the assistance and indeed to the 'utterance' of the Spirit. Yet in the very same message we may either at the time, or in retrospect, wish that we had not said certain things or expressed ourselves in a certain way for fear of being misunderstood or of giving offence. We realise that it was of the flesh, our words and not God's word. After all Peter tells us that 'if anyone speaks, he should do it as one speaking the very words of God' (I Pet 4:11) and does not seem to distinguish between the different kinds of speaking – preaching, teaching, or prophesying. All Christian speaking then would seem to be 'mixed' partly of God, partly of us; and it is for this reason that prophecy also is to be tested and weighed.

For similar reasons I confess some unhappiness with the emphasis or tradition in some renewal circles which decrees that a prophecy is often cast in the first person singular as though it was all the direct words of God through the individual to the congregation. It can become rather stereotyped in a quasi-Authorised Version sort of way. David Atkinson writes concerning this:

> The common use of the first person singular in charismatic congregational prophecy today has no New Testament precedent, and would not seem to be of the essence of prophecy, but

rather to be a behavioural habit developed within the subculture. Its use severely complicates the duty of weighing and discerning the truth of the prophetic words, by clothing the message in a form which seems to claim a divine authority which, if it is such, puts the words outside the area of discussion.[21]

To this we could also add three points. First, though Old Testament prophets did use the first person, they also prefaced their words with 'Thus saith the Lord.' Second, Old Testament prophecy is anything but stereotyped, and exhibits a great variety: in Malachi the vast majority of verses are the direct words of God, whereas Jonah is mainly narrative and the actual message to Nineveh is only half a verse (Jonah 3:4). Or we might compare Zechariah with his remarkable visions, and Hosea making vivid application from his own sad marital experience. Our stereotype more likely stems from imitation than inspiration. Third, it seems almost disrespectful to test and weigh what purport to be the words of God and not men. But the Bible tells us we must, so that it would be even more disrespectful not to obey what we know to be the written word of God, commanding us to test what may be no more than the fallible words of man.

For this reason a missionary society, happily encompassing some widely varying views — even some who believe that the gifts ceased with the apostolic age — has asked its members to refrain from phraseology that appears to claim direct revelation and to substitute such wording as 'I believe that what God is saying to us in this situation is . . . .' In this way it is hoped that members can be true to their convictions, but not break fellowship with those holding different views.

Visions and Dreams

These also may be a form of revelation *apokalupsis*, a word used of contributions made to worship in I Cor 14:26. The

Joel passage quoted by Peter on the day of Pentecost says that: 'your old men shall dream dreams and your young men shall see visions.' This is to be one mark of the new age heralded by Pentecost. There are six occasions in Matthew's gospel when God spoke through a dream: first to Joseph (1:20), then to the wise men (2:12), then again to Joseph telling him to flee (2:13), again telling him to return (2:19), and again to Joseph telling him to go to Galilee (2:22). The Lord also spoke to the wife of Pilate in a dream (27:19). Paul speaks of 'visions and revelations from the Lord' (II Cor 12:1). Ananias of Damascus is spoken to by the Lord in a vision, and is told 'in a vision' that Saul had seen a man named Ananias come and place his hands on him to restore his sight (Acts 9:10-12). Cornelius had a vision of an angel (Acts 10:3), and Peter saw the vision of the great sheet full of unclean animals (Acts 10:17). It was through a vision of the man of Macedonia (Acts 16:9) that Paul was called to enter Europe. On three later occasions Paul was given encouragement in dreams and visions (Acts 18:9; 23:11; 27:23).

It would then be ridiculous to suggest that God did not use this way of communicating with his servants, or even with non-Christians. At times of revival, however, it is possible for people to go overboard over this and to regard all dreams as being visions from God. In the recent Borneo revival this happened, and all manner of wild dreams were reported until a leading Christian, Joseph Balan Seling, provided a Bible study on dreams including authentic ones (as we have mentioned above), but at the same time reminding them that there are false dreams (Jer 23:25-32; 27:9), but also that some dreams may arise from an overactive mind or may be meaningless (Eccl 5:3, 7). In view of the danger of limelight-seekers offering sensational dreams as a status symbol, it was refreshing to hear from Bishop Festo Kivengere that in the East African revival the leaders might suggest that the dreamer had eaten too much cheese before going to sleep the previous night! The same cautious testing is needed for dreams and visions as for other kinds of revelations and prophecies.

We see then that prophesying and teaching and encouraging overlap, so that some prophecy may be little different from relevant teaching, where the Lord has shown what the real issues are. I have even heard a lecture described as having been 'prophetic' in character. At the same time, it seems that Scripture does allow for the possibility of revelations, dreams and visions, and we must not therefore despise prophesyings (I Thess 5:20-21). However, because of the danger, not only of counterfeit, but of the mixed nature of present-day prophecy, we must carefully and cautiously test the content before we accept it as being genuinely from God. Light varies not only in wavelength, but in intensity, and the same would seem to be true of the grace that shines to give *charismata*. There seems no reason why prophets in this New Testament sense should not exist today, provided they are also diligent students, soaked in Scripture, living by every word that comes from the mouth of God, and able to apply it to contemporary situations.

Teachers

What a gift this is! That sense of delight that spreads through a whole congregation, and you hear the rustling of leaves (in what were once trees, but have been cut down to print Bibles!) as a fellowship finds itself blessed through the faithful teaching of the Word of God, where the Spirit has given gifts to the teacher. And what a heavenly sense of elation in the teacher who knows that the Lord has made him a teacher, and knows that the Lord has been pleased again to bless the people of God through his ministry, with all those years of hard study now shown to be so worthwhile. We read, for example, that Ezra the scribe 'had devoted himself to the study and observance of the Law of the Lord, and to teaching its decrees' (Ezra 7:10). Far away in Babylon this man had studied and prepared himself for some future ministry. Later we get the marvellous description of that great day when the returned exiles assembled as one man in the square before the Water Gate. 'They told Ezra the scribe to bring out the Book of the Law of Moses ... He read it aloud from daybreak till noon ... .' (Neh 8:1-3) On that great day of spiritual revival and rededication of the congregation to the Lord, how Ezra must have rejoiced that the Lord had prepared him through all those years of study, when captive in an alien land, and that now all was being used for God's glory.

The gift of teaching, overlapping with prophecy and encouragement, is the primary God-given means of edifying the church and building up the body. It is one of the most exciting gifts and one with the greatest possibilities on the missionary scene today. If you really want to be stretched as a teacher, then a fascinating variety of opportunities awaits you in cross-cultural missionary service. Get rid of that mental image of the tedious transfer of information from the notes of the lecturer to the notes of the student without passing through the minds of either! Stop thinking of teaching as imparting information so that people can pass examinations!

Let me remind you that some charismatics get excited over prophecy, tongues, and healing, and less so over teaching: yet Scripture says that this is third after apostles and prophets. There is a feebleness of much that passes for teaching, no less in some avowedly 'charismatic' churches, which seems odd when it is the third of the gifts that are placed in order in I Cor 12:28. Teaching is something that we should get excited about also, for good teaching is thrilling and a great stimulus to faith.

The Great Commission contains two different words for teaching (Matt 28:19-20). The first word is 'make disciples', showing that this was 'teaching with a view to commitment'. The second tells us that those baptised as disciples are then to be taught to obey everything that Jesus had commanded them, that is 'teaching with a view to behavioural change'. Traditionally too much Christian teaching is pulpit soliloquy, because nobody ever checks up to see if anyone takes any notice, or if the teaching produces any action.

It is not surprising that the gift of teaching is included in nearly every list of gifts. The ministry of Jesus was principally a teaching ministry, and Acts refers to the 'apostles' teaching' (Acts 2:42); indeed, the opponents of the gospel did their utmost to stop them teaching (Acts 4:2-18; 5:28). Barnabas soon went to fetch Paul from Tarsus, and the two of them taught the church there for a whole year. One teacher became two teachers, rapidly became five teachers (Acts 13:1) and later became many more (Acts 15:35). This multiplication of teachers is so different from the static 'one-teacher school' pattern of so many congregations (even when they have rows of trained teachers sitting in the pews).

After controversy about whether or not apostles and prophets are to be seen as foundational gifts no longer needed by the church, it is a considerable relief to find that nobody has any doubts about the need for the Lord to give teachers to the churches although many still undervalue them. My friends who ask whether 'the gifts' may be used almost certainly do not regard preaching and teaching as being contained within their inverted commas. They are in error, then, for there is no doubt that teaching is one of the most prominent of the spiritual gifts referred to in the New Testament. In the Old Testament it is mentioned before worship as a responsibility of the priests and Levites: 'He teaches your precepts to Jacob and your law to Israel. He offers incense before you and whole burnt offerings ... ' (Deut 33:10); and again in the prophets we find the same emphasis: 'For the lips of a priest ought to preserve knowledge, and from his mouth men should seek instruction – because he is the messenger of the Lord Almighty.' (Mal 2:7) Worship can be an abomination to God in the absence of sound teaching: 'I hate, I despise your religious feasts; ... though you bring choice fellowship offerings, I will have no regard for them. Away with the noise of your songs! I will not listen to the music of your harps.' (Amos 5:21-23)

The Word of Wisdom and the Word of Knowledge

Reference to the NIV shows that a great deal has been built upon the accident of King James language, for I Cor 12:8 now speaks of 'the message of wisdom, to another the message of knowledge'. The word *logos* used here may be used to mean 'preaching' or 'teaching' (as well as 'word'). The same word has traditionally been translated as 'preaching' in I Cor 1:18 − 'the preaching of the cross'. Here is yet another place where the accident of a familiar English translation has influenced popular understanding of these gifts as a kind of Christian clairvoyance. If the translation from the beginning had been 'teaching of wisdom' and 'teaching of knowledge', the misunderstanding might have been avoided. The table of lists of gifts (pp 26-27) will show that in that list there is no other reference to the gift of teaching, an omission which does suggest that this translation is actually the correct one. Stephen Clark, who belongs to the Roman Catholic charismatic community in Ann Arbor, says:

> The first two gifts which St Paul mentions are teaching gifts: the *utterance of wisdom* (sometimes translated 'the word of wisdom') and the *utterance of knowledge* (sometimes translated 'the word of knowledge'). They are special inspirations by which God works through one person to give understanding to another person or to a group of people ... . St Paul, when he was speaking about the utterance of knowledge, almost certainly does not mean a special knowledge of facts that a person could not have known otherwise.[22]

In other words, this is an excellent illustration of teaching being built upon the accident of English translation to build a whole superstructure that really has no biblical support. I am not saying that the Lord may not be pleased on some occasion to give an insight into some problem or illness. What should be questioned is the practice whereby week after week suggestions are made that there is 'somebody present with migraine' or 'somebody present with a bad back' (in all but the smallest groups of people the probability is pretty high) and this is called 'a word of knowledge'. Let's not pretend that this is a biblical idea.

Bridge and Phypers also point out the problem of accepting that these gifts refer to

> uttering an inspired wise saying in some sort of church meeting which involves a problem or points the way forward in a hitherto intractable situation ... once it is accepted that any individual Christian may give infallible, detailed guidance to a church or other Christian group, the door is opened to all sorts of problems and difficulties.[23]

They go on to point out the further danger if a group of Christians is engaged in a takeover bid for control:

> a 'word of wisdom' might seek to reverse carefully thought-out policies of the existing leadership. If the 'word of wisdom' is then followed, some degree of leadership will thereafter almost inevitably lie in the one credited with the inspired gift ... . If the 'inspired word' is not obeyed, then the leadership can be denounced as 'unspiritual' and a new call to the membership for loyalty and obedience will often result in division.[24]

In other words, gifts are meant to edify or build up the

body of Christ, and it denies their purpose if they can be manipulated to give any kind of justification for splitting congregations.

John Owen says, 'the word of wisdom is nothing but wisdom itself . . . ' and then links it with the promise of the Lord Jesus (Luke 21:15) 'that I will give you a mouth and wisdom' which their adversaries will not be able to resist. Stephen displayed this gift (Acts 6:10). Thus Owen sees this as a special gift for the defence of the truth of the gospel.[25]

Even the words 'wisdom' and 'knowledge' are not easily distinguishable. C K Barratt says rather blandly: 'It is not clear how (or indeed whether) a word of wisdom and a word of knowledge are to be distinguished.'[26] It's no good writing him off because we may think we know how we should distinguish the way we use those words in renewal circles today. Barratt is facing the problem of defining them in terms of the way they were used in the New Testament. Some argue that wisdom has a practical character in the Old Testament, whereas knowledge may be speculative, so that the first would represent a practical discourse — mainly ethical instruction — and the second an exposition of Christian doctrine. However, Barratt points out that in I Corinthians itself, in the immediate context, 'knowledge' is connected with practical matters (e g 8:10) about food offered to idols), while 'wisdom' is speculative (e g 1:21). Then he suggests that Paul is varying his speech and using a parallelism, as he does earlier with 'gifts', 'ministries', and 'operations' (I Cor 12:4). There seems every reason for caution in being too dogmatic about what was meant by these words in Paul's day, and still greater caution in arbitrarily identifying them with present day experiences.

To sum up, then, it seems unwise to insist arbitrarily on experiential grounds that a 'word of wisdom' must mean what we say it means. It seems safer and greater wisdom to establish the meaning of words from their biblical usage and therefore to include these two categories in that section of the spectrum of grace which we call teaching.

Pastors

As we have already seen, the absence of the article before 'teachers' in Eph 4:11 suggests that 'pastor/teachers' are one group and not two.[27] This is the only reference in the Bible to a 'pastor' or 'shepherd' being a gift *(doma)*. All of the other references to this word *(poimen)* in the New Testament are either to literal shepherds who find sheep or run away, or to the Lord Jesus himself as the great Shepherd (Heb 13:20; I Peter 2:25). However, the use of the verb *(poimaino)* makes shepherding the responsibility of the apostle Peter, and Peter himself teaches elders to shepherd the flock (I Peter 5:2), while Paul similarly instructs the Ephesian elders (Acts 20:28). There is a link also with the word 'overseer', for the shepherd stood on some prominent knoll from which he might literally see over the flock and thus notice any marauding wolves. We may therefore explain the solitary reference to the pastoral gift in combination with the gift of teaching, because it is a general function of the local church elder, who both oversees and teaches.

While on the subject of ministry in the local church, we should notice that the office of deacon corresponds with those spiritual gifts variously listed as helps, service, giving and showing mercy; while both overseers and elders could be identified with the administration of Corinthians and the 'he who presides' of Romans. Thus the combination teacher/pastor suggests that in the local congregation, a pastor would be one of a number of teaching elders.

In days when churches are changing very fast, when pastors are making many innovations, and when long-standing churchmembers are feeling threatened and even leaving congregations they have loved for many years, it is good to remind ourselves that there is an optimum speed for moving a flock. The shepherd who tries to get his flock to move too fast, will find them dash off and scatter in all directions. And the wise pastor will not treat the congregation as though they were no more than literal sheep — it is only a metaphor!

He Who Encourages

This gift is mentioned specifically as a spiritual gift only once, in Romans 12:8: 'if it is encouraging, let him encourage'. Here is yet another instance where we can be misled by the present nuance of the English word to think that this means having the gift of cheering people up. A word study of the way the New Testament uses the word will help.

When Paul and Barnabas were in the synagogue in Pisidian Antioch, after the reading from the Law and the Prophets, the leaders asked them: 'Brothers, if you have a message of encouragement *(logos parakleseos)* for the people, please speak.' (Acts 13:15) When Paul is writing to Timothy about his ministry, he writes as follows: 'devote yourself to the public reading of scripture, to preaching *(te paraklesei* so perhaps better 'the exhortation') and to teaching *(te didaskalia* so better 'the teaching') (I Tim 4:13). The definite articles, then, seem to imply that following the official reading of the lectionary, from the Law and the Prophets, there then commonly followed 'the exhortation', that is an exposition based upon the readings, much as today in some Anglican churches preaching is based upon the Epistle and Gospel readings that precede it. It seems that the synagogue pattern was followed also in the early churches.

This throws light on other passages. It is what the Lord Jesus did in the Nazareth synagogue after the reading from the prophet — he gave the 'exhortation' that day (Luke 4:21ff). John the Baptist was doing the same (Luke 3:18). Peter on the day of Pentecost 'with many other words he urged them, and he pleaded *(parekalei)* with them ... ' (Acts 2:40), was exhorting them to repent and be converted. He was not cheering them up. The writer to the Hebrews uses the word on several occasions: 'you have forgotten the *parakleseos* that addresses you as sons' (Heb

12:5) and 'I urge you to bear with my word of *parakleseos*' (Heb 13:22).

Thus, when we are told that Joseph of Cyprus was nick-named by the others 'Barnabas', which means Son of En-couragement (Acts 4:36), he was, (according to this Hebraism) *huios parakleseos*, that is, characterised by exhor-tation or encouragement. It means much more than that he had a warm cheerful nature and an ability to cheer up others. It is more probably an acknowledgement that he had such a gift for hortatory teaching that it became his nickname! Having been chosen by the Jerusalem church to go to Antioch, as soon as he arrived he manifested his gift and showed why they chose him: 'he encouraged them all to remain true ... ' (Acts 11:23). Later, after he and Paul had made many disciples in Galatia, we read once more: 'They returned to Lystra, Iconium and Antioch, strength-ening the disciples and encouraging them to remain true ... ' (Acts 14:22). In classical Greek the verb was used repeatedly about pep talks given to soldiers before battle, and there is something of this in the apostles' 'encourag ing', for the next verse reads 'We must go through many hardships to enter the kingdom of God'.

We can now understand why there is the overlap between this gift and prophecy, which, as we saw, is re-peatedly said to 'encourage' (as in Acts 15:32; I Cor 14:3, 31). There is more to prophecy than reporting upon a 'revelation', for there will be exhortation or exposition based on it. We can also see why this was a missionary gift essential to the church planting apostles as they encour-aged young congregations to become independent of them, particularly when facing spiritual battle and fierce per-secution.

It would be helpful if there were more emphasis upon cultivating this particular spiritual gift. As with prophecy and teaching, it is to be seen as closely linked with God's word already given; and following the reading of Law and Prophets, as it seems to have done, demonstrates the rel-evance of Scripture, and the application of it to the present situation of the Church.

Evangelists

This gift is also mentioned only once (Acts 4:11) as one of those human gifts given by Christ to his people *(domata)*, although Philip is also referred to specifically as 'the evangelist' (Acts 21:8), presumably to distinguish him from the apostle of the same name. Timothy is also commanded to do the work of an evangelist (II Tim 4:5).

We may well wonder why this gift is not more frequently mentioned, for it would seem an obvious and essential one. It is perhaps because it was necessarily exercised by church planting apostles, as a study of the verb 'evangelise' in Acts makes clear. The verb is used 15 times in Acts and 20 times in Paul's epistles. Some significant usages are no less than five occurrences used to describe Philip the evangelist's ministry (Acts 8:5, 12, 25, 35, 40); the ministry of Paul and Barnabas (Acts 13:32; 14:7, 21; 15:35) and later Paul's European mission (Acts 16:10; 17:18). The use of the verb supports the suggestion that this gift was one especially evidenced by the apostles as they planted churches. It gives us another classic example of the overlap of spiritual gifts: apostles need to be evangelists, though not all evangelists are apostles.

A further reason is that the word 'herald' or 'preacher' may be a synonym for evangelist, so that, for example, Paul twice describes himself as 'a herald and an apostle ... and a teacher' — in that order in both instances (I Tim 2:7; II Tim 1:11). John Stott quotes Alan Richardson as saying that the work of a herald 'is the telling of news to people who had not heard it before'[28] and that is what an evangelist does. The concept of a herald reminds us that *evangelion*, the gospel, means not just any old 'good news' but more specifically good news about the king authoritatively proclaimed by the herald.

We should notice that the ability to herald the good news with authority is not just the adoption (or imitation?) of well tried techniques to bring people to a decision, but is specifically a gift from the ascended King to his people (Eph

4:8). If good evangelists are rare enough in Western countries, the challenge of the need is greater still in missionary situations, where missionary church planters need to be able to evangelise effectively in another language, showing the relevance of the gospel in another culture. We need to pray that the King will send more heralds, give more national evangelists to churches throughout the world, including those who may be effective on radio and television, as well as in public meetings of varying sizes.

Faith

This gift again is mentioned only once, in the I Cor 12:4-11 list and again in the following chapter: 'if I have a faith that can move mountains, but have not love I am nothing.' (I Cor 13:2)

The immediate context of the reference in I Cor 12 places faith in close association with the gift of healings and the effecting of miracles, so that we may again see the principle of overlap functioning here, since both healing and miracles require a particular exercise of faith. We see that Elijah in Mount Carmel, for instance, manifested a most remarkable faith that the Lord would choose to vindicate himself in a power confrontation with the prophets of Baal (I Kings 18).

We must however not identify 'faith' either with brash presumption (every non-Christian who attends will be converted at tonight's meeting) or the subjective hunch that someone is going to be healed, which, when unfulfilled, is blamed upon the unbelief of those praying, or, even more cruelly, upon the lack of faith of the person for whom healing is sought.

When the Lord Jesus healed people there were occasions when the one to be healed was expected to express faith (Matt 9:28; 15:28); in other instances it was the faith of others which was important (Matt 9:2; Mark 5:36); in other cases, faith is not requested but is given as reason for healing (Matt 9:22; Luke 7:50; 17:19; 18:42; John 4:50); and there are yet other instances when faith is not mentioned at all — just the grace and kindness of the Lord (Luke 5:12; 7:15; 13:12).

Can we find further guidance in Scripture itself what 'faith to remove mountains' might mean? In Matt 17:20 the lack of faith to move mountains was behind the disciples' failure to cast demons out of the boy. In Mark 11:21-25, in the context of the cursing of the fig tree, there is the further reference to a mountain-moving faith exercised in prayer accompanied by forgiving others. In Luke 17:3-6 a mulberry-tree-moving faith is required to go on forgiving a brother who sins against you and asks for forgiveness seven times a day.

There is a rugged realism about faith in this teaching of the Lord Jesus. The biblical evidence may be scanty, but in addition to needing such faith for exorcism, it is needed generally for 'believing prayer' and especially in forgiving those who sin against us. This is an unexpected conclusion, for we tend to think of such 'faith' for remarkable exploits, and not the down-to-earth forgiveness of difficult people.

Yet in a discouraged group, there are men and women of 'faith', who take firm hold of God's promises, and are a blessing to the whole group, because of their firm expectation that the Lord will be pleased to reveal his saving power in difficult situations.

Healing

Gifts of healing are referred to in all three Corinthian lists, in each case together with the gift of miracles. The healing miracles of Jesus may be seen as the credentials of his Messiahship (Luke 7:20-23). In the same way healings and miracles could also be regarded as 'the signs of an apostle' (Heb 2:3-4; Rom 15:19; II Cor 12:12).

Peter healed the lame man at the Beautiful Gate (Acts 3:6). Following the prayer for such demonstrations (4:30) we are told that 'apostles' performed many miraculous signs and wonders (2:43; 5:12, 16). Peter also healed the paralytic Aeneas (9:34) and raised Tabitha (9:40). He was also himself miraculously released from prison (12:7ff).

Stephen and Philip also 'did great wonders and miraculous signs' (6:8) and 'great signs and miracles' (8:6, 13) which show that the ministry was not restricted to the Twelve.

Paul It is instructive to notice where healing miracles are recorded in the various cities in which the apostle ministered in Asia and Greece: in Iconium 'Paul and Barnabas spent considerable time there, speaking boldly for the Lord, who confirmed the message of his grace by enabling them to do miraculous signs and wonders.' (Acts 14:3); in Lystra Paul healed a crippled man (Acts 14:8); in Jerusalem Paul and Barnabas reported on 'the miraculous signs and wonders God had done among the Gentiles through them' (Acts 15:12); in Philippi Paul exorcised the slavegirl from the divining spirit (Acts 16:8); at Corinth (II Cor 12:12); at Ephesus God did extraordinary miracles through Paul (Acts 19:11); at Troas Paul raised Eutychus from death (Acts 20:10); and in Malta Paul cured Publius' father of dysentery, and then others (Acts 28:8).

Two comments on these miracles are in order: First, while no healing miracles are reported from Antioch, Derbe, Perga, Thessalonica, Berea, Athens, or Rome, it does not seem to have been Luke's purpose to show that such miracles happened everywhere, and within the limits of the space he had, he has given us sufficient indication. Second, the miracles seem to have been performed chiefly by the apostles, and Stephen and Philip as those appointed by the apostles. It does not seem that they were performed generally. Why else was it sufficiently remarkable and significant to report the miraculous signs performed by Paul and Barnabas (Acts 15:12)? This means that a strong case can be made for the suggestion that this *charisma* was restricted to apostles and other church leaders, and not exercised by believers generally. Paul's question: 'All are not workers of miracles, are they? All do not have gifts of healings, do they?' (*NASB* I Cor 12:29) is thus especially pointed.

However, one exception to this would be Ananias who went to Saul of Tarsus, and placed his hands on him, for healing of his blindness and so that he might be filled with the Holy Spirit (Acts 9:10-18). He is simply described as a disciple: God makes his own rules, and thus it would seem that God is not limited to using leaders.

It has been pointed out that these New Testament healings were 'instantaneous, without failure, irreversible, covering all manner of diseases, dependent on the charisma of the healer not the faith of the seeker, and so a sign to the unevangelised'.[29] Even if this contrast with much that is claimed as healing today is a bit overdrawn, it is a valid point to be considered carefully. Turner's summary statement is helpful:

> We merely insist, on the one hand, that the idealised picture of apostolic healing drawn from some sections of Acts should not be taken necessarily as *representative* (certainly not of *charismata iamaton* operating *outside* the apostolic circle, (I Cor 12:28ff) and, on the other hand, that serious modern testimony points to phenomena so congruent with some apostolic experiences that only *a priori* dogmatic considerations can exclude the possibility that New Testament *charismata iamaton* have significant modern *parallels*.[30]

Some ill thought out views about healing suggest that obedient Christians ought never to be sick. But in New Testament times, miracles of healing do not seem to have been available as a first-century Health Service, such that any Christian falling sick might *automatically* have expected to be healed. If this had indeed been the case, we might expect to find no record of Christians ever being sick, except perhaps as divine chastening or punishment (I Cor

11:30). This is not the case. Timothy is told to use wine for medicinal purposes ('because of your stomach and your frequent illnesses' I Tim 5:23). Epaphroditus was sick to the point of death, but God had mercy on him (Phil 2:27). Trophimus was not healed by the apostle, but left sick at Miletus (II Tim 4:20). Paul himself speaks of his own 'weaknesses' (II Cor 12:7-10), and this may also be implied in earlier references to 'despairing of life' and 'being afflicted in every way' (II Cor 1:8, 9; 4:8-12; 11:24-27).

The general teaching of the Lord Jesus is that God has not settled for some simplistic: 'Goodies will be blessed, and baddies will suffer' solution. Quite the reverse, God allows no discrimination. He makes his sun rise and his rain fall on just and unjust alike. 'He fills your hearts with joy', says Paul to the pagans at Lystra (Acts 14:17). The corollary of this is that Christians experience misfortune and illness, just like other people. Those who build on the sand experience flood, storm and tempest. Do those who build on the rock find the sun shining all day long? No, they also suffer, but built on the rock they do not fall. So Christians are not automatically immune to viruses, nor do they escape the results of their own or other people's careless driving. Michael Green writes with robust good sense when he says:

> God does not always choose to heal us physically, and perhaps it is as well that he does not. How people would rush to Christianity (and for all the wrong motives) if it carried with it automatic exemption from sickness! What a nonsense it would make of Christian virtues like long suffering, patience and endurance if instant wholeness were available for all Christian sick! What a wrong impression it would give of salvation if physical wholeness were perfectly realised on earth while spiritual wholeness was partly reserved for heaven! What a very curious thing it would be if God were to decree death

> for all His children while not allowing illness
> for any of them![31]

There has been a huge spate of literature concerning this gift in recent years. (See for example *We Believe in healing*.)[32] In *Miraculous Healing*, however, Henry Frost — the first Home Director of the China Inland Mission in North America — wrote one of the finest and most balanced treatments of the subject at a time when the Christian and Missionary Alliance had been placing an overemphasis upon healing:

> The Lord is to be recognised as having the right
> of way over the life of the saint, so that He may
> do what He will with him ... not ruthlessly,
> but lovingly and tenderly ... Christ will choose
> health, strength and length of days for some of
> his saints; He will choose the opposite for
> others of them.[33]

I have little doubt in my own mind that the Lord can and does heal today. My difficulties lie with people who assume that Christians have a right to healing (until their inevitable terminal illness), or that we have some method whereby we can force God to heal. Whether with or without the use of medical means, we should not hesitate to offer prayer for the miraculous intervention of God's grace.

During my overseas service I was on four occasions asked to lay on hands for healing in accordance with the procedure outlined in James:

> Is anyone of you sick? He should call for the
> elders of the church to pray over him and
> anoint him with oil in the name of the Lord.
> And the prayer offered in faith, will make the
> sick person well; the Lord will raise him up.
>
> (James 5:14)

The principle of the request of the sick person is important, though in 1957 I laid hands on an Egyptian baby at the request of his Coptic Christian parents on board ship en route for Asia. In 1970 with others I laid hands on a 60-year-old colleague at his request and in 1975 on a Chinese colleague over 70 at the time: both these two men are still alive and preaching at the time of writing. The fourth was a much younger person suffering from acute rheumatoid arthritis in 1972. He continued to suffer with great cheerfulness and died seven years later. Both the older men were extremely ill, and while there is no proof that they were healed *because* we laid hands on them, (or that they would certainly have died, had we not done so, for who but God knows that), I do believe that God in his mercy healed both those men in answer to our prayers on their behalf. I mention this to show that I do have experience of the Lord's healing in obedience to James 5:14, and to indicate that when requested by the sick person, I believe we are correct to follow the practice.

Miracles

Under this heading I want to consider New Testament miracles which cannot be included under 'gifts of healing'. The miracles of Acts do not seem to include any 'nature miracles' like the plagues in Egypt or the Lord Jesus stilling the storm or feeding the multitude (unless we regard Philip as miraculously levitated to Azotus in Acts 8:39, 40). However, Paul asks, 'Does God give you his Spirit and work miracles among you because you observe the law, or because you believe what you heard?' (Gal 3:5)

What Kinds of Miracles Do We Find in Acts?

Miracles of Judgement The deaths of Ananias and Sapphira his wife (Acts 5:5, 10) and the blindness of Elymas (Acts 13:11) are two solemn examples, both of them, incidentally, apostolic.

Raising of the Dead Peter raised the dead Tabitha at Joppa (Acts 9:40), and Paul later appears to have raised Eutychus at Troas (Acts 20:10). Again both are apostles, and we have record of them doing this only once each in a lifetime.

Miracles of Deliverance On three occasions apostles were miraculously liberated from prison, twice by an angel of the Lord (Acts 5:19; 12:7) and once by an earthquake (Acts 16:26),[34] perhaps also from shipwreck and snakebite (Acts 27:24; 28:5).

Miracles of Exorcism (It is problematical whether to include these here or under healing, but again these two gifts are related and the principle of overlap would again seem to hold.) The healing of those 'tormented with evil spirits' (Acts 5:16) by the apostles (5:12) is recorded from Jerusalem. Philip also exorcised demons in Samaria (8:7) where 'with shrieks, evil spirits came out of many'. Paul healed the slave girl possessed by a spirit by which she predicted the future (Acts 16:18), and exorcism formed part of his ministry in Ephesus where 'the evil spirits left them' (Acts 19:11). The interesting event that follows tells of Jewish exorcists who endeavoured to cast out evil spirits 'In the name of Jesus, whom Paul preaches . . . .' This shows that Christian exorcism is not merely the use of a magic formula, which any might use.

It is again significant to notice the extent to which this gift seems to have been exercised by apostles rather than others. It is this kind of biblical evidence which can be used to suggest that the gift of miracles has 'long since ceased' because there are no apostles who need to give their authenticating credentials today. In the Old Testament there are periods when there are many miracles — two great outbursts — in the days of Moses and Joshua and again in the time of Elijah and Elisha. There are also long periods when there did not appear to be any miracles — in the time of the patriarchs and in the period of David and Solomon. It is thus possible to argue that the period of Jesus and the apostles was a third great outburst of miraculous signs, but that today miracles are again very rare.

While noting the relative infrequency of non-healing miracles, we should still keep our minds open to the possibility of God's intervention. What else do we expect when we ask him to supply financial needs, for example? In pioneer missionary situations also, there are times when there is confrontation with demonic religion, or need for an authenticating witness of the missionary (apostolic) witness. While the stories from Timor in Indonesia were certainly exaggerated by certain sensationalists, it does seem likely that some miraculous intervention of God was truly experienced initially.

Working in northern Japan, a somewhat resistant area, I myself and others known to me prayed for the gift of miracles so that an impression might be created and converts come pouring into the churches. The Lord seemed to ask me whether, in praying for this, I was capable of handling miracles in these days of the media, with television reporters wanting some repeat performance. 'Missionary Heals Ten' headlines might or might not help. I have never known missionary prayer to receive the gift of miracles answered affirmatively, though the Lord does sovereignly deliver from danger, heal illness, provide for financial needs, and arrange circumstances in ways that can only be called miraculous. An interesting object lesson took place in Hokkaido town where there had been some well-attended meetings conducted by a Japanese evangelist. Several hundreds of people came and scores were counselled. A month or so later, a further series of meetings was advertised by another group imitating almost exactly the style of posters and leaflets used for the evangelistic campaign earlier. However, these advertised: 'Come and see miracles performed rapidly one after the other.' One might have imagined that such a meeting would be a great draw for curious people. In the event attendance was very small indeed compared with the evangelistic meetings held earlier. Sophisticated modern people are sceptical, and afraid of being taken in by ingenious illusionists. Doubtless the curious were temporarily entertained, but without any lasting result. John Owen has a strong warning:

> God might on some occasions ... put forth his power in some miraculous operations .... But the *superstition* and folly of some ensuing ages, inventing and divulging innumerable miracles, false and foolish, proved a most disadvantageous prejudice against the gospel, and a means to open a way unto Satan to impose endless delusions upon Christians.[35]

In spite of all this, we cannot close our minds to the possibility that the Lord may be pleased to intervene, when he sees it to be proper and appropriate, and for his glory and the blessing of his children. A recent book by Donald Bridge says helpfully:

> *We must not turn anecdotes into rules* .... If we cannot dismiss the *Acts* stories as *'not for today'*, does this mean that they should be repeated in our lives and in our churches *every day?*[36]

It is in the nature of miracles to be very rare events: if they became everyday events, they would cease to be noticeable as miracles and their value as *signs* would be lost. C S Lewis' superb book *Miracles* (Centenary Press: London, 1947) deserves to be much better known than it is.

Demon Possession and Oppression

It seems important to discover all we can about this from Scripture itself, and make a brief biblical survey of the symptoms of attack. We find the words 'demon' (21 times), 'evil spirits' (6 times), and 'unclean spirits' (25 times) are used almost interchangeably with one another concerning the same evil spirit, and it does not seem that any distinction is intended.

Such demons, unclean or evil spirits are said to be responsible for dumbness (Matt 9:32; 12:22; Mark 9:17; Luke 11:14), blindness (Matt 12:22) and a woman being bent double (Luke 13:11). Other symptoms are often violent, including crying out and convulsions (Mark 1:23; 3:11), foaming at the mouth and grinding teeth (Luke 11:39), or casting oneself upon the ground or into fire or water (Matt 17:15; Luke 4:35; 9:38-43). This suggests that demon possession is evidenced by obvious outward symptoms causing deafness, dumbness, blindness, or some other physical complaint or manifestly violent bodily actions and cries. There do not seem to be instances in the New Testament of people being quietly or discreetly demon-possessed!

It should also be noticed that individuals are not permitted to claim diminished responsibility due to demon possession. Jesus says:

> For from within, out of men's hearts come evil thoughts, sexual immorality, theft, murder, adultery, greed, malice, deceit, lewdness, envy, slander, arrogance and folly. All these evils come from inside and make a man unclean.
>
> (Mark 7:21-23)

James says:

> But each one is tempted when by his own evil desire, he is dragged away and enticed.
>
> (James 1:14)

We should not therefore blame upon the devil and demons things which the Word of God attributes to 'the flesh' or 'the heart of man'.

To the vexed question of whether a Christian may be demon-possessed or not, one can only reply that — first — there is no record of this happening to a Christian in Scripture; second, that II Cor 6:15-16 suggests that it is impossible for someone who is in-dwelt by the Holy Spirit of God to be possessed by demons: 'Or what fellowship can light have with darkness? What harmony is there between Christ and Belial?'; and third, that Luke 11:24-26 speaks of the unclean spirit finding the 'house' empty, and bringing back seven others, so that the last state is worse than the first. The context is that of the power of Jesus to overcome 'the strong man' and throw him out. Once the Lord Jesus is in possession, who will bind and overpower him?

This is not to deny that a Christian may be demon-oppressed or exposed to demonic attack, but to say that a Christian might be possessed by an evil spirit is a denial of the power of Christ to keep his own safe. It seems theologically unacceptable to suggest that the Holy Spirit might be driven out of his own temple by evil spirits.

There is a difference between recognition of the war on the saints (Rev 13:7) by the spiritual forces of wickedness (Eph 6:12), on the one hand, and a superstitious fear of pictures of dragons, Satanist curses and the like. We are not dualists who believe that the powers of God and of darkness are equally matched. Satan is a defeated foe, and we have been given authority over him and his minions:

> I have given you authority to trample on snakes
> and scorpions, and to overcome all the power
> of the enemy; nothing will harm you.
>
> (Luke 10:19 and context)

Service

Helps *(antilempseis)* is a gift mentioned only once (I Cor 12:28) and is a rare word not found elsewhere in Scripture, although the verbal form is found in Acts 20:35 'We must *help* the weak' and also Luke 1:53ff 'He has filled the hungry with good things, but has sent the rich away empty. He has *helped* his servant Israel.' (Also II Maccabees 8:19 mentions help in battle.)

The basic idea seems to be helping the poor, needy, and sick. This is the work for which the Seven were initially appointed, to provide for the physical needs of widows in Jerusalem (Acts 6:1,2). However, quoting a recently discovered papyrus, Bittlinger says it was a technical word in banking referring to the administration of money.[37] If this is correct, then it involves helping the poor by almsgiving, and so yet another overlap with the 'contributing to the needs of others' and also the 'showing mercy' of the Roman list (Rom 12:8). It may be then that we have here the most direct reference to treasurers of church accounts, and more particularly the care of the needy poor.

There is a pleasing note in Cranfield about the gift of showing mercy:

> A particularly cheerful and agreeable disposition may well be evidence of the special *charisma* that marks a person out for this particular service ... for he will recognise ... an opportunity to love and thank him who can never be loved and thanked enough.[38]

It would also seem proper to associate this gift with the serving *(diakonia)* mentioned by Peter, as well as those referred to in Romans, together with the allusion in I Cor 13:3 'If I turn all my property into morsels of food (literally)'. Direct biblical reference to these gifts is scanty (but see p116 on the ministry of widows), and they do not seem to have attracted the same interest as more spectacular gifts.

In ancient Corinth, north of the theatre, lay the Asclepieion, a temple devoted to the Greek God of Healing — Aesclepius — who was alleged to reveal himself to his devotees through dreams and visions. Some of the finds from this site are facsimiles of the affected parts and are stored in the Asclepieion Room in the Corinth museum. As well as plaster models of arms and legs, there are also casts of what the apostle euphemistically calls 'unpresentable parts'. One might wonder whether it was sight of these in Corinth, that prompted this illustration of parts of the body when writing to the Corinthians.[39] Paul's point is that there are parts of the body, essential to procreation, which are modestly concealed, but are none the less important (I Cor 12:22-26). Paul insists that these more modest gifts, less in the public eye, are none the less manifestations of God's grace, just as 'charismatic' as other gifts more obviously displayed. We too need this reminder. The work of treasurers, typists, houseparents, visitors, and welcomers-at-doors are also manifestations of grace and need the help of the Spirit.

It is good to remember this when attending a large meeting, for at first sight we are prone to be grateful to the well known speaker, and perhaps the distinguished chairman. But a planning committee conceived and organised the meeting; a secretary wrote letters. Somebody else designed the posters and the programme, and someone else planned music and arranged for it to be played. Others cleaned the hall and arranged the chairs and platform. Someone else lit the boiler. Others arranged the flowers, microphones, and other paraphernalia. A whole team has prepared food for refreshments and served it. Others welcome visitors, hand out programmes or hymnbooks, show people to their places, and organise some kind of bookstall. If the speaker had to do all that on his own, he would soon realise what a relatively small amount of the work done has been his — in terms of time commitment or in energy many have given more than he has. What a large number of people have to cooperate to produce a good meeting. If there are other presentations, panels, interviews, soloists, audiovisuals and drama, there need to be still more planning, rehearsing, and arrangement of material.

We need to have a more biblical view, then, of the way in which the different limbs and organs co-operate. We often talk as though the mouth was the only organ of significance, but Paul uses the word *charismata* in a much more thoroughgoing way than we do. It is these more practical and essentially non-verbal gifts which keep the church growing and provide evidence of the credibility of the church to the world at large. They are not only non-verbal, but also unspectacular, yet none the less expressions of serving grace through the Spirit.

Administration

Some years ago I was travelling on a Greek airline, and handed the official handbook, idly read the words *ho kubernetes kai to pleroma*. I recognised two New Testament Greek words and wondered why the airlines would write about 'the steersman and the fullness'? Reference to the more easily understood English instructions revealed that 'The captain and crew' welcomed me aboard. The word for 'gifts of administration' *kuberneseis* is related to the word *kubernetes* used in modern Greek for a captain or a pilot, and in the New Testament for a ship's captain (Rev 18:17) or helmsman (Acts 27:1). It is from this word that our English word 'cybernetics' derives. Just as the helmsman steers or pilots the ship, so those with 'gifts of direction' should guide the progress of a congregation. It is this spiritual gift which is manifested by church moderators, bishops, and elders and by directors of parachurch societies. The same word is used in the Old Testament (Prov 1:5; 11:14; 24:6) of 'counsellors' where according to Kittel the best translation would be 'clever direction'.

The music 'Sailing the Seas Depends upon the Helmsman' was current in Mainland China recently. The importance of the helmsman increases in time of storm, and it is ironic that in Acts 27:41 the ship ends up hitting the rocks! The spiritual gift is needed to give the congregation a clear sense of direction. C S Forester's Captain Hornblower series provides an apt illustration of a leader who is always thinking ahead, and planning for fresh eventualities in directing the course of his ship! Because of lack of this gift, some congregations seem to travel round in circles on the same spot, as it were, without any sense of goal and direction. So this is an essential and exciting gift for leaders.

The gift appears to be related to the gifts of 'leading' or perhaps 'presiding', *prohistamenoi*, found in Rom 12:8 and I Thess 5:12, and also used in the vernacular of that time for 'officers'. Therefore, in the chart, 'administration' and 'leading' are on the same horizontal level. Presumably it could also include the administrative aspects of the work of the church performed by church secretaries and others, though they might be subsumed under gifts of service.

While we commonly endeavour to produce just one comprehensive doctrine of the 'ministry' from the New Testament (and fail to come up with any clear answer!), it is significant to note the variety of words used to describe church leaders in the different epistles and Acts.

Acts:	*presbuteroi* ('elders', as in the Jewish synagogue)
	episkopoi ('overseers' as a synonym for elders in 20:28)
Romans:	*prohistamenoi* ('he who leads' or 'presides' in 12:8)
	diakonos ('deacons' of Phoebe 16:1)
Corinthians:	*kuberneseis* ('administration' in I Cor 12:28)
Ephesians:	*poimenas kai didaskalous* ('pastors/teachers' 4:11)
Philippians:	*episkopois kai diakonos* ('overseers and deacons' 1:1)
Thessalonians:	*prohistamenoi* ('those who are over you' I Thess 5:12)
Pastorals:	several references to overseers, elders, deacons (and women?)
Hebrews:	*hegemonoi* ('leaders' in 13:7, 17, 24; cf Acts 15:22)

Studying each place separately, we discover a remarkable variety of titles, descriptions, and offices, which may explain why it is difficult to be quite so dogmatic about 'the New Testament church order' as though there were only one. All seemed to have had leaders, but what they called them seems to have been a matter of indifference. Oddly enough, as students of Acts know, the cities had different names for their secular leaders also. There is room in the New Testament for a degree of cultural variety in what names we actually give to our church leaders.

Leadership style for the church is described by the Lord Jesus as different from autocratic Gentile secular leadership (Matt 20:25-28) and from ostentatious Jewish religious leadership (Matt 23:8-12). It is to be marked by humility and service of the saints, and is to be exercised not by ordering others about, but by example (John 13:14-15; I Peter 5:3). It is a pity that so much attention has been directed to names and hierarchical schemes, and so little to leadership style. The enthusiasm for applying secular business techniques based upon the profit motive to Christian church life seems to me to be as suspect as the gentile leadership style against which Jesus warned his disciples. Certainly, it should not be accepted uncritically.

This word *kuberneseis*, related to the word for steersman, is a useful reminder that so many churches become programme-orientated instead of goal-orientated, and have little sense of progress or direction. A fuller appreciation of leadership as *steering* might do a great deal to set our churches on a clearer course towards perfection.

Discernment

This gift is referred to only once (I Cor 12:10), immediately before the reference to different kinds of languages and interpretation of languages. The need for this gift was indicated at the introduction of the problem of discernment in I Cor 12:1-3. Gentile Christians with a pagan background are reminded that before conversion they had been 'moved' to speak by evil spirits associated with idol worship. How were they to tell whether someone was speaking by the Spirit of God, or by some evil spirit counterfeiting authentic inspiration? The danger of self-inspired prophets, spurious tongues, or even deliberate misleading of Christians by evil spirits counterfeiting genuine communication makes this gift of great importance (ironically, even to 'anti-charismatics').

On close examination there are far more illustrations of the exercise of this gift in the narrative of Acts than I had at first realised. First, there is Peter discerning the deceptive hypocrisy of Ananias and Sapphira (Acts 5:3), and discerning the false motivation of Simon Magus (Acts 8:20), at a time when *charismata* were being very remarkably manifested. Paul exposes the wickedness of the false prophet Bar-Jesus or Elymas in Cyprus (Acts 13:10), and discerns that even though the words uttered by the slave girl are factually correct, they spring from the evil spirit by which she is possessed (Acts 16:18).

The further reference in John's First Epistle (I John 4:1) reminds us of the importance of discerning whether messages brought to us in the church are from men, from Satan, or truly from God himself. This gift helps us to identify whimsy and subjective fancies dressed up as visions or revelations, fanaticism, errors, cynicism, or other distortions of Christian truth.

This is no new problem. Jeremiah dealt with it in the Old Testament when men spoke lies and dreams in the name of God (Jer 23:16-40). It was a problem at the time of the great evangelical awakenings in New England about which Jonathan Edwards wrote so much:

> Satan seeks to delude revived believers by immediate suggestions and inspirations, inviting them to conclude that all the thoughts and texts which come into their minds unbidden must be

messages from God. He seeks to lead them into imprudences of all sorts in the heat of their zeal.[40]

It is always worthwhile to learn from the experience of the past, and an actual quotation from Jonathan Edwards expounding I John 4:1-6 will help:

Another rule to judge of spirits may be drawn from ... the sixth verse ... if by observing the manner of operation of a spirit that is at work among a people, we see that it operates as a spirit of truth leading persons to truth, convincing them of those things that are true ... for instance if we observe that the spirit at work makes men more sensible than they used to be, that there is a God, and that he is a great and sin-hating God; that life is short and very uncertain; and that there is another world; that they have immortal souls, and must give account of themselves to God; that they are exceedingly sinful by nature and practice; that they are helpless in themselves; and confirms them in other things that are agreeable to some sound doctrine; the spirit that works thus operates as a spirit of truth; he represents things as they truly are ... and therefore we may conclude, that it is not the spirit of darkness that doth thus discover and make manifest the truth.[41]

Much more recently David Watson wrote in similar vein, not so much about the content of an utterance, but about the character of the person through whom such utterances may be brought to the church:

The tests are clear:
(a)   Is Jesus Lord of that person's life? 'No

> one can say "Jesus is Lord" except by the Holy Spirit.
>
> (I Cor 12:3)

(b)   Is Jesus Christ acknowledged as Perfect Man and Perfect God? 'By this you know the spirit of God: every Spirit which confesses that Jesus Christ is come in the flesh is of God'.

(I John 4:2)

(c)   Is there a measure of true godliness and holiness about the person? 'Every sound tree bears good fruit, but the bad tree bears evil fruit ... Thus you will know them by their fruits'.

(Matt 7:15-20; cf II Peter 2:1-3)

David then went on to say that in addition to these more objective tests: 'there can be a spiritual ability, given by the spirit, to distinguish between the spirits.'[43]

Not all Christians are able to discern between that which is real and that which is counterfeit. Bishop Festo Kivengere of Uganda, talking of the East African Revival, told me of an aged African lady who after a long, loud and uncharitable diatribe from someone, remarked quietly:, 'I did not see the marks of the crucified hands in what you said.' There is always the Simon Magus problem of the person who wants to climb onto the bandwagon and be one of the in-group. It is the old Brethren problem in a new guise: to distinguish between a brother who has something to say (from the Lord) and a brother who has to say something (so as not to be left out).

We need this gift in our churches. If someone speaks in an unknown tongue, and someone else offers a translation, how does anybody discern whether this is a true translation that is offered, apart from a gift of discernment? It is true that some Christians are naive, gullible, and eager for the sensational; but it is also true that others of us are cautious, conservative, and critical. We suspect that this crucial gift of discernment is not confined to the latter group! It requires a God-given ability to discern what is authentic, wholesome, and God-glorifying. All congregations of Christians need warm, spiritual, respected members who will exercise this function in the body.

Speaking in Languages

I confess I have had problems with my experience of people who break into the middle of worship in some unknown language, even when it is followed by another person offering some kind of interpretation. It seems such an odd roundabout way for the Lord to communicate with us: why does he not use straightforward prophetic utterance instead, when we can all judge and weigh what has been said? It somehow does not seem at all like the God that I believe in. Having said that, I must respect the fact that some very sincere Christians seem to feel that speaking in languages is genuine and find it helpful. But you will understand why I want to raise questions about whether what is spoken of in I Corinthians is necessarily to be identified with what happens in some churches today. We assume that they must be the same thing, but are we sure we have got it right?

Reference to the chart shows that this *charisma* is referred to in all five of the Corinthian lists, though in none of the others. How are we to understand this word *glossa*? 'The noun *glossa* has only two known meanings, namely the organ in the mouth and a language.'[44] A cardinal rule in biblical interpretation is that identical expressions have identical meaning, so there is strong linguistic presumption that the 'languages' referred to in Acts 2:4-11 have the same meaning also in I Cor 12-14. After all, if on the day of Pentecost, Jerusalem was full of people speaking many different languages, then it is surely not too far-fetched to expect that in a large cosmopolitan seaport like Corinth there would not infrequently be overseas visitors: Parthians, Medes, Elamites, dwellers in Mesopotamia, Judea, and Cappadocia, Pontus and Asia, Phrygia and Pamphylia, Egypt, districts of Libya around Cyrene, Cretans, Arabians and visitors from Rome! In such a multilingual port, there must have been occasions when someone preferred to speak in his own native language, rather than in bad Greek, and that this might then be incomprehensible to the predominantly Greek-speaking congregation. It is true that one is understood by God (I Cor 14:2), and that such a person edifies himself (v 4) because he knows what he is trying to say. It is quite unintelligible to everyone else (v 6) 'how will anyone know what you are saying? You will just be speaking into the air' (v 9). That is why in the absence of an interpreter, such a person is to be silent. 'If there is no interpreter, the speaker should keep quiet in church and speak to himself and to God.' (v 28).

There are a variety of possible views:

Unpopular Literal Interpretation

I suspect that many readers may never have questioned before whether the Corinthian experience might have been of such a straightforward nature. Everything that Paul says seems to me to be explicable in terms of what is still today a missionary problem of communication across the normal linguistic barriers. Some years ago I was invited to speak to a predominantly Hokkien-speaking congregation in Taiwan. What language would I speak? How about English? No good: we have no one who is able to interpret it well enough. How about Japanese? That's fine. The older people all understand it already, and we have some good interpreters for the benefit of the younger Mandarin-educated young people. Surely that is not just a twentieth-century problem? Problems of language must also have occurred sometimes in the Mediterranean world of the first century. We know that Paul and Barnabas were in difficulties in Lystra, when they could not understand the Lycaonian language (Acts 14:11-14).

Thus, even if you disagree, I hope you will accept that it seems sensible to understand the references to gifts of language and of interpretation *literally*. I have spent much of my life in missionary situations where communication is a constant problem. An essential part of a missionary's qualification and training is his gaining fluency in one or more new languages. For the first three or four years of service, the time involved in studying and learning language and the restrictions of inability to speak language well enough to communicate Christian truth are major factors. In some countries two years' full-time language study is mandatory. Even after that someone may still be speaking at the level of a not very coherent teenager. For tribal work in the Southern Philippines people have to learn three languages: Tagalog, the national language; Cebuano, the trade language of Mindanao, and the language of the particular tribe they will be ministering to. In Thailand or even in Indonesia, someone working among tribal people will certainly need to learn two languages. The same is true in French speaking Africa

We always need the *charis* of God and the help of the Holy Spirit when preaching, but speaking personally I pray all the more for that help when I have to speak in Japanese: there are many aspects that are learned, or stem from natural ability, but missionaries need the 'gift of languages' if they are to be effective ministers of the Word of God. If we understand the gift in this sense, then it would be an essential gift for taking the gospel to all nations. On this understanding I Cor 14 is dealing with what happens in a linguistically mixed congregation when no other person present can interpret into the majority language. Rereading of the text shows that Paul's stress is upon intelligibility, especially in verses 6-23.

What is perhaps fatal to this view is that while it helps explain some scriptural verses, it seems quite impossible to understand others in this way. Verse 14 is one such example: 'For if I pray in a language, my spirit prays, but my mind is unfruitful.' If, however, as I have been suggesting, the language is known to the speaker, his mind should fully understand. It seems difficult, too, to understand why the Corinthians should be so pleased with themselves for speaking in other contemporary languages in their meetings. 'Look how many races and nationalities we have in our church!' There are difficulties in the literal interpretation as there are in the others.

The 'Charismatic' Interpretation

How do we understand the interpretation that has been current among Pentecostal churches for eighty years, and which has become accepted in some renewal and restoration churches in more recent years? It cannot be denied that during worship services in those circles people are used to hearing languages that are not understood, as well as the interpretations that are then offered. In Pentecostal churches in periods of worship it is not uncommon to hear many of the congregation all praying at once and many of them uttering sounds not corresponding with known languages. No interpretation is asked for or expected. This does not seem to have any direct correspondence with I Cor 14, but it could be argued that 'praying in tongues' is different.

This leads us naturally to the current view that 'praying in tongues' is an entirely private and personal exercise. Packer describes it objectively as:

> A God-given capacity for prayer and praise, valuable, because as experience shows, it enables worshippers to sustain and indeed heighten moods of adoration, penitence, petition and intercession in a way they could not do otherwise. The gift is regarded as mainly, though not entirely, for private devotional use. Subjec-

tively, it is a matter of letting one's vocal chords run free as one lifts one's heart to God ... [45]

Goldingay gives the following justification:

> Paul, then, is essentially negative in his evaluation of tongues in relation to the congregation. But he makes it clear that he does not mean total rejection of the gift. 'Thank God I am more gifted in ecstatic utterance than any of you,' he says, and 'I should be pleased for you all to use the tongues of ecstasy' (vv 18, 5a); we should not try to explain away these expressions of appreciation. Paul in fact makes clear why he places a certain value on tongues.
>
> 1. Tongues really is a way of 'talking with God' (v 2) ... while the fact that words cannot be understood by men is a reason for playing down the use of the gift in public, this fact is less of a disadvantage when the gift is used in private, for God, to whom prayer or praise in tongues is addressed, can understand them.
>
> 2. Tongues really 'is good for' (RSV edifies) 'the speaker' (v 4) ... Tongues thus seems to fulfil a function not unanalagous with that of art or music for some ...
>
> 3. Tongues ... is not a higher, but a lower form of prayer (v 14) but is a real form of prayer. It is neither the key to holiness nor the peak of spiritual achievement (as the Corinthians show) — but it may be a valuable feature of elementary and basic Christian experience, a real blessing from God at that level. [46]

The Neutral Medium of Expression View

Glossolalia is not unique to Christianity. It is found in Islam, Hinduism and was found with the dancing madness of the Middle Ages. This is not to denigrate it but to say that in itself it is neutral, like singing hymns or chanting, neither of which is unique to Christianity either. The medium is neutral of itself: everything depends upon its content: singing may be vulgar, salacious, or just banal; or it can be exalted and spiritual because its content is thoroughly Christian. Tongues may be described as *free vocalisation*.

> *Free vocalisation* (glossolalia) is a term used to denote the production of connected sequences of speech sounds, not identified by the speaker as a language known to him ... which sounds to an average hearer like an unknown language ... . We may define *Tongues Speech* as Free Vocalisation for religious purposes by one competent in his native tongue.[47]

On this understanding *Free Vocalisation* is in itself neutral, exactly as singing is, and depends upon its content.

Turner quotes W J Samarin's serious linguistic research saying that the samples prove to be 'strings of syllables made up of sounds taken from among all those that the speaker knows, put together more or less haphazardly.'[48] On this understanding 'tongues speaking' is a technique which can be developed by anyone who wants to do so. Some charismatics instruct others:

> Though sometimes starting spontaneously in a person's life, with or without attendant emotional excitement, *glossolalia* is regularly taught (loosen jaw and tongue, speak nonsense syllables, utter as praise to God the first sounds that come, and so forth) and through such teaching it is in fact *learned*.[49]

I confess myself to be increasingly less sympathetic to the present understanding of 'tongues' whether in public or in private, but then we are all influenced by our background, and to me it seems like totally unnecessary mystification, and I am not a very mystical person. The following points need to be considered carefully:

First, the overall drift of I Cor 14 is to *discourage* the Corinthian practice, whatever it was. It is turning the whole thing on its head to use that passage to justify something that may (or may not) be the same thing.

Second, we should give more weight to Paul's objection that glossolalia is a hindrance to evangelism, because it will seem weird and spooky: *'Will they not say that you are out of your mind?'* (I Cor 14:23). Televising of churches speaking in tongues has precisely this effect, which the Bible regards as undesirable. If signs and wonders are thought desirable because they are alleged to assist evangelism, then we should take seriously this apostolic warning about the negative effects that hearing 'tongues' can have upon unbelievers.

Third, even if we may disagree as to whether I Cor 14 speaks about the private exercise of glossolalia, it cannot be denied that what Paul says imposes strict limits on its public use.

Fourth, it is questionable whether I Cor 14 is about 'private tongues' at all.

> But one thing is clear: *prima facie*, Paul is discussing *public* use of tongues throughout I Cor 13, 14, and it is neither necessary nor natural to refer any of his statements to glossolalia as a private exercise. Charismatics often explain 14:4 ('he who speaks in a tongue edifies himself … ') and 18 ('I speak in tongues more than you all') in terms of private glossolalic prayer, but exegetically this is a guess that is not only unprovable but not in fact very plausible.[50]

Fifth, it cannot be too strongly emphasised that Paul asks: 'Do all speak in tongues?' (I Cor 12:30) in the form that requires the answer 'No!' It is therefore quite arbitrary to divide Christians into two classes of 'haves' and 'have nots' in relation to this or any other gift. Please reconsider what was written earlier in this book about the way in which gifts are given by God and received by men. If the whole concept that we should 'seek' gifts is a misunderstanding, then it must have relevance in relation to the gift of tongues also. Even if the Corinthian passages did enjoin us to 'seek', it would mean that the congregation is told to seek the gifts that it needs corporately, rather than that individuals should seek them for themselves. And Paul does not seem overeager for them to pursue after 'tongues speaking'.

Interpretation of Languages

This gift is referred to in three lists, and as might be expected, always in association with the gift of languages. In the worship of the synagogue there was always an 'interpreter', who, when the Scriptures were read in ancient Hebrew, would translate them into contemporary Aramaic. Jews were thus quite familiar with an 'interpretation' being given. Thus Aaron is described as being Moses' interpreter, and Papias refers to Mark as 'interpreter' of Peter. These wider uses of the word strengthen the case for *glossai* being translated as meaning (foreign) 'languages'.

The word is also used in Luke 24:27 of Jesus explaining to them what was said in all the Scriptures concerning himself, and again it is used in John 1:38, 42; 9:7 and Acts 9:36 with the ordinary meaning 'translated'. The natural meaning of 'translate' in its general biblical usage seems to imply that the interpreter must have a direct understanding. It is not difficult to discover beforehand whether there is somebody present who is competent to translate Japanese or Cantonese, and if there is not to keep silent. This all seems relatively straightforward.

If no name can be given to a language, then it is not possible to know until afterwards whether it can be interpreted or not, and this makes it harder to obey the biblical injunction. It is often said in charismatic circles, that the 'interpreter' of tongues need not understand the 'language' himself, but is speaking out the words which God gives him. Thus after an utterance has been given incomprehensible to the congregation, then a second utterance is given by someone who does not understand it either, but is especially illumined to give the message or translate the prayer in plain language. This gives rise to the question, then, why *two* people are needed as mouthpieces at all, for the first person does not seem to be really needed. It is alleged that tongues plus interpretation is the equivalent of prophecy, but if this is really so, it is difficult to understand why I Cor 14 seems to have been written to demonstrate the superiority of prophecy. Frankly again this understanding of what is meant by 'interpretation' sounds like special pleading. Even more does the argument that by delivering it in a foreign language first, it serves to emphasise and undeline its importance. To me this seems like more mystification of what might be understood in a more straightforward fashion.

Missionary experience again is that when one cannot speak in the native tongue of the people one is addressing, the interpreter needs the unction of the Spirit, just as much as does the original speaker. Those of us who have frequently been ministered to by speakers using languages unfamiliar to us, but made a blessing to us by gifted interpreters, have no doubt that this is a grace-gift. The plain meaning of 'interpret' from one known language into another requires serving grace ministered by the Holy Spirit.

Footnotes

[1]David Aune, *Prophecy in Early Christianity and the Ancient Mediterranean World* (Eerdmans: Grand Rapids, USA,

1983); Wayne Grudem, *The Gift of Prophecy in First Corinthians* (University Press of America: Maryland, 1982); Max Turner, 'Spiritual Gifts Then and Now', *Vox Evangelica*, vol XV (1985); K S Hemphill, *The Pauline Concept of Charisma* (Cambridge Ph D Dissertation, 1976).

[2]Turner, *op cit*, p 10.

[3]John Goldingay, 'The Church and the Gifts of the Spirit', *Grove Booklets on Ministry and Worship*, No 7 (1972): p 11.

[4]See Michael Green, *I Believe in the Holy Spirit* (Hodder & Stoughton: London, 1975), p 169.

[5]F F Bruce '1 and 2 Corinthians', *New Century Bible* (Oliphants: Basingstoke, 1971), p 134.

[6]Alec Motyer, *New Bible Dictionary* (IVP: Leicester, 1962), p 1045.

[7]Earle Ellis, 'The Role of the Christian Prophet in Acts', in Gasque and Martin, *Apostolic History and the Gospel* (Paternoster Press: Exeter, 1970), p 55.

[8]John Stott, *Baptism and Fullness* (IVP: Leicester, 1975), p 100.

[9]Turner, *op cit*, p 15.

[10]Grudem, *op cit*, p 43.

[11]David Atkinson, 'Prophecy', *Grove Booklets on Ministry and Worship*, No 49 (1977): p 20.

[12]Turner, *op cit*, p 16.

[13]Aune, *op cit*, p 339.

[14]Turner, *op cit*, p 10, referring to Grudem, *op cit*, pp 115-143.

[15]Stephen Clark, *Spiritual Gifts* (Dove: Pecos, New Mexico, 1969), pp 18-19.

[16]Goldingay, *op cit*, p 7.

[17]Green, *op cit*, p 170.

[18]Ellis, *op cit*, p 58.

[19]*ibid*, p 51.

[20]Anonymous, *The Charismatic Movement in the Church of England* (CIO Publishing: London, 1981), p 22.

[21]Atkinson, *op cit*, p 22.

[22]Clark, op cit, pp 9-11.

[23]Donald Bridge and David Phypers, *Spiritual Gifts and the Church* (IVP: Leicester, 1973), pp 48-49.

[24]*ibid*, p 50.

[25]John Owen, *The Holy Spirit* (Sovereign Grace Publishers: Grand Rapids, 1971), p 866.

[26]C K Barratt, *A Commentary on the First Epistle to the Corinthians* (Black: London, 1971), p 285.

[27]See Gerhard Kittel, *Theological Dictionary of the New Testament*, vol VI (Eerdmans: Grand Rapids, USA, 1972), p 497.

[28]John Stott, *The Preacher's Portrait* (Tyndale: London, 1961), p 30.

[29]Turner, *op cit*, p 48. Compare also with J I Packer, *Keep in Step with the Spirit* (IVP: Leicester, 1984), p 213.

[30]Turner, *op cit*, p 49.

[31]Green, *op cit*, p 176.

[32]Ann England, *We Believe in Healing* (Marshall Pickering: Basingstoke, 1982).

[33]Henry Frost, *Miraculous Healing* (Marshall, Morgan and Scott: Basingstoke, 1951), p 114.

[34]For recent experience of deliverance of missionaries see A E Glover, *A Thousand Miles of Miracle in China* (Pickering & Inglis: Basingstoke, 1919).

[35]John Owen, *The Holy Spirit* (Sovereign Grace Publishers: Grand Rapids, 1971), p 887.

[36]Donald Bridge, *Signs and Wonders Today* (IVP: Leicester, 1985), p 137.

[37]Arnold Bittlinger, *Gifts and Graces: Commentary on I Corinthians 12-14* (London: Hodder & Stoughton, 1967), p 70.

[38]C E B Cranfield, 'Romans', *International Critical Commentary* (T & T Clark: Edinburgh, 1979), p 627.

[39]See Andrew Hill, *Journal of Biblical Literature*, XCIX (1980): p 437.

[40]J I Packer, 'Jonathan Edwards and the Theology of Revival', *Increasing in the Knowledge of God* (Puritan &

Reformed Studies Conference Papers: London, 1961), p 26.

[41]Jonathan Edwards, *Works*, vol II (London, 1840), pp 266-269.

[42]David Watson, *One in the Spirit* (Hodder & Stoughton: London, 1973), p 92.

[43]*ibid*.

[44]John Stott, *Baptism and Fullness*, p 112.

[45]Packer, *Keep in Step with the Spirit* (IVP: Leicester, 1984), p 177.

[46]Goldingay, *op cit*, pp 21-22.

[47]Turner, *op cit*, p 44.

[48]W J Samarin, *Tongues of Men and Angels* (Macmillan: London, 1972), p 81.

[49]Packer, *Keep In Step with the Spirit*, p 10.

[50]*ibid*, p 208.

CHAPTER 5

WHICH SPIRITUAL GIFTS MAY WOMEN RECEIVE?

When I was a member of the Overseas Missionary Fellowship, two-thirds of my fellow workers were women, half of whom were married, half unmarried. They were committed to an extent that frequently made me feel humble and full of admiration. Many of them exercised most fruitful ministries, enjoying opportunities much greater than anything that might have been offered to them, had they remained in Britain.

Since I have been at the London Bible College, it has been my task to teach both men and women in the same classes (roughly one-third being women). In a class called 'Learning to Preach and Teach' students are required to submit message outlines each week. I observed that the outlines submitted by women were often better than those that came from men: that the women in question usually had some experience of teaching already certainly gave them an advantage. But nothing in the work submitted by women suggests that they are incapable of teaching, or that the standard of their material is rarely as good as men's. It was my observation that on average they were at least as good as, and often better than, the men in the same class, many of whom were training for the pastoral ministry.

I find, then, a remarkable discrepancy between my experience of the abilities of women in Christian work, and the degree of opportunity that is given to women to use their spiritual gifts in this country's churches. Why is this?

It probably represents the same *cultural* trend that confines women to the lower rungs of the professional ladder.[1] It must be added that it also reflects the conviction of some sincere Christians that there are *scriptural* reasons for restricting the ministry of women, that certain gifts are not given to women at all, and that therefore they must not be allowed to exercise them, even if they seem to have them!

It therefore seems an important exercise in a book about spiritual gifts to ask what examples there are in the Bible not just of persons in general exercising spiritual gifts (recognising that such statements may well include women as well as men), but of women being particularly singled out or mentioned by name as exercising some of the spiritual gifts discussed earlier in this book. We shall follow the order in which those gifts were discussed in the main body of the book.

Apostles

It seems self-evident that when Jesus chose the Twelve to be with him they were all men. Women were among his disciples, and indeed he and the others were supported by the generosity of certain women (Luke 8:2-3). Mary sat at his feet and learned as a disciple, a remarkable development during a period when rabbis generally seemed to have felt that women were not capable of theological study (Luke 10:39). Indeed, in view of the way in which the band of disciples travelled around together it probably would have been culturally inappropriate for women to have been part of the apostolic band.

However, there is one reference which may describe a woman as an apostle. 'Greet Andronicus and Junias, my relatives who have been in prison with me. They are outstanding among the apostles.' (Rom 16:7). Some of the manuscripts read 'Junia' in the feminine, and it is more likely that a male ending was added to a female word than the other way round. Lest it be thought that this is a wild and biassed assertion, two quotes from Cranfield's magnificent commentary on the Greek text will suffice:

> Their [Sanday and Headlem] statement that 'Junias ... is less usual as a man's name' is misleading, since the truth seems to be that, apart from the present verse, no evidence of its having existed has so far come to light ... In view of this last fact, it is surely right to assume that the person referred to was a woman.

> ... it is much more probable — we might well say, virtually certain — that the words mean 'outstanding among the apostles', that is, 'outstanding in the group that may be designated apostles'.[2]

There is no doubt that Chrysostom understood a female to be so designated: 'how great was this woman that she should be numbered among the apostles', he wrote.[3] She was not one of the Twelve, but of that much wider company including Paul, Silas, Barnabas, Timothy, and Epaphras who are so described, being apostles of the churches rather than of the Lord. It can still be argued that a man was intended, but it has to be freely admitted that the case for Junia being a woman is much stronger, and that this would then be an exception to the general rule.

Prophets

In the New Testament three men are named as prophets, Agabus (Acts 11:28; 21:10), Judas, and Silas (Acts 15:32). The four *daughters of Philip* (Acts 21:9 the same context as Agabus) are not actually named. But *Anna* is called a prophetess (Luke 2:36-38), and we are to understand that both *Elisabeth* the mother of John (Luke 1:41-45) and *Mary* the mother of Jesus (Luke 1:46-55) were prophesying. There are also the two specific references to women prophesying, in the Joel quotation (Acts 2:17-18), and the passage about head covering (I Cor 11:5), which specifically refers to women prophesying as well as praying. If there is still some doubt about the Junia reference showing that women could be apostles, there can be no doubt at all that women did prophesy and could also bear the designation of prophetess in the New Testament, as well as in the Old. *Huldah* was consulted about the book of the law discovered during the reign of Josiah, even though they could have consulted Jeremiah (II Kings 22:14). *Deborah* is also described as a prophetess (Judges 4:4). There can be no doubt that this gift is clearly given to women.

Teachers

There is no example of a woman being named in the Scriptures as being a teacher or having the gift of teaching. The five men named as prophets and teachers in Antioch (Acts 13:1) include Paul, who twice describes himself as a teacher (I Tim 2:7 and II Tim 1:11).

Older women are, however, specifically commanded to teach younger women (Titus 2:4). Taken in conjunction with I Tim 2:12, this is usually taken to imply that women may not teach men. However, it is clear that the gifted *Priscilla* (whom Paul describes as his colleague or fellow worker Rom 16:3) was involved in instructing Apollos, whose faith was manifestly defective. Certainly she did this with her husband and in private, but her name is mentioned first (Acts 18:26).

How are we to understand the apparent ban on women teaching men in I Tim 2:12? When taken out of the whole context and quoted as 'I suffer not a woman to teach a man' it seems quite decisive. However, a decision has been made to read two Greek words as simply 'woman' and 'man', when elsewhere the same two words are translated, for example, 'Wives obey your husbands'. The passage can equally well be read as 'I do not allow a wife to teach or domineer over her husband'. The word 'domineer' or even 'contradict' is a strong word with a nasty flavour, and needs to be taken with 'teach' rather than separated from it. Thus it could in that context be taken to mean that a wife can teach as long as she does not domineer over her husband. In any event it is improper for a wife to domineer over her husband, and equally improper for a husband to behave like that towards his wife, instead of loving her and sacrificing himself for her (Eph 5:25). Some have felt that the strength of the word *(authentein)* is such that there must have been some specific unpleasant case in mind in Ephesus when Paul wrote, and that the command was thus an *ad hoc* one rather than a general command.

But there is a much stronger and more general argument that has to be faced. We have seen in our discussion of gifts in general that there is overlapping between different gifts like that of colours in a spectrum. We have seen in the general discussion of prophecy that it does overlap with teaching, e g, 'You may all prophesy one by one, so that all may learn and all may be encouraged.' (I Cor 14:31) We have seen already in the discussion above that there is very strong New Testament evidence for women prophesying, indeed it is a mark of the new age that 'your daughters' and 'maidservants' will prophesy as well as 'your sons' and 'menservants'. If they may prophesy in the church, then 'all may learn' and that must inevitably include men.

Those of us men who are married learn a great deal from our wives. It is a poor marriage relationship where a man learns nothing from his wife. The Puritans suggested that the husband and the wife each had a major role in blessing and instructing each other mutually. 'There is a great deal of duty which husband and wife do owe to one another; as to *instruct, admonish,* pray, watch over one another, and to be continual helpers to each other.'[4]

I have already remarked on my experience of the teaching gift actually being exercised by women: why does the Holy Spirit give this gift if he does not intend that it should be exercised by women? It is sometimes allowed in Brethren circles, for example, that a woman may teach other women and children of both sexes both in Sunday School and in her own family, but not adult men. The inconsistency of this view has been pointed out by many writers, of whom the most recent is Elaine Storkey.

> A quick reflection will soon recognise that if a woman is unfit to impart truth to those of maturity, reflection and wisdom, it would hardly be wise to allow her free access to the immature, trusting and formative minds of children.[5]

When arguing the biblical case for the ministry of women, it is sensible to avoid 'cultural' arguments, for this suggests that we are setting aside what the Bible teaches on cultural grounds. (For example, though it might have been appropriate for Paul to make such a ruling in ancient times when the vast majority of women were illitcrate, it is no longer applicable in a day when women in general are better educated and capable of being teachers in both schools and universities.) This is not an illegitimate argument, but it could be regarded as an attempt to avoid what is regarded (wrongly in my view) as a self-evident ban on the ministry of women. Thus, tempting though this argument is, it may be wiser to forego using it, and to argue the case purely on exegetical grounds as I have sought to do in this chapter. It is my conviction that we can demonstrate that the Scriptures themselves do allow very considerable opportunity for the ministry of women, much more than is currently allowed by many — one might say on twentieth-century cultural grounds!

We have seen that there is strong biblical evidence for women exercising the gift of prophecy, one example of a female being called an apostle, and other examples of women exercising some kind of ministry, notably in Rome and Philippi. This may be paralleled by the teaching gift still currently manifested by many spiritual Christian women, most especially in the overseas mission field. Therefore, not because we want to question Scripture, but because Scripture must be consistent with itself, we have a responsibility to take a fresh look at passages like I Tim 2:11-15 which are notoriously difficult, in order to ascertain that we have understood their original meaning correctly. Are women always necessarily more easily deceived than men (who are so easily deceived about women!)? And how are women saved in or through childbearing? And why are the Greek words *aner(andros)* and *gyne(gunaikos)* — normally translated 'husband' and 'wife' — here made 'man' and 'woman'? It would cause far less problem if we translated: 'I do not permit a wife to lecture and domineer over her husband ... ' (and it could be translated that way) rather than I do not allow a woman to teach ... '. None would feel it right for a wife to treat her husband that way (or for the loving husband described in Eph 5:25 to treat his wife that way either!). Such a difficult passage must be treated and expounded with caution and humility, recognising that we only 'know in part'. It is quite inconsistent to limit the ministry of women on the basis of part of the passage while owning honestly that we are very foggy about what the rest of it means! If we do not understand the context clearly, we must hesitate to insist that the verse in question must mean what we say it means!

There is one argument which might be dismissed as 'cultural' — which I think merits careful consideration none the less. It is not arguing on the basis of greatly improved education for women in the modern world. It points out rather that during our New Testament period, there were no officially recognised New Testament documents to determine authentic doctrine. It was the oral testimony of the apostles which was normative. Subsequently, with the fixing of the canon, there was from then on an external authority by which the teaching both of men and of women could be tested and regulated. From that time onwards, both men and women had a much simpler task, because the content of their teaching was determined by the written record of the apostles witness to Jesus and his teaching.

Pastors

There is no example of a woman in the New Testament being named or described as a pastor, but then there is no example of a man being so described either! There are only general statements about the gift of pastor/teacher, or of elders 'pastoring' – as we have seen in the earlier discussion. There are two comments worth making, however.

First, experimentally. Women seem much more interested in pastoral counselling than men do (attend any course and see for yourself) and are often more perceptive and caring than men. Looking back I notice how often I have tried to help a person, because a woman has quietly suggested that so and so might appreciate the chance to talk. Am I alone in feeling that women are more sympathetic and easier to talk to than men?

Second, biblically. While women are never actually referred to as pastors, there are situations where women do seem to be in a position of leadership in a local church. For example, there is the church in the house of Aquila and Priscilla, and perhaps even more significantly 'the church in the house of Nympha' (Col 4:15). We know that the church in Philippi appears to have met in the house of Lydia. It has been suggested that these women acted as patronesses or sponsors to the civil authorities, pledging the good behaviour of the Christian group for whom they were acting as guarantor.[6] The interesting example is that of the deacon (*diakonos* while masculine in form is used as neuter in gender, common to both men and women) *Phoebe*, who is also described as *prostatis*. This word is much stronger than the usual rather feeble translation of 'helper' or 'succourer'. In the masculine form it is used in early Christian literature of Christ as the *guardian* of the church (I Clement 61:3; 64:1). This double description of Phoebe must be taken seriously: a man so described would be thought of as being a leader in the local church.

As we have seen the word 'pastor' is not used specifically of either sex by name, but if the church was meeting in a woman's house, or if a woman was acting as patroness of a Christian group, one might well suppose that she might exercise some measure of pastoral care, even though she would not have been a one-man-band 'pastor' as such. Most of the problems about the ordination of women are problems about 'ordination' and the one-man-band-omni-competent-pulpit-primadonna view of the ministry. In a plural leadership, it would seem a matter of common sense that some of those leaders should be women.

He Who Encourages

Is this expression ever used specifically of a woman? It is never used of any named person, male or female. However, the nickname 'son of encouragement' was given to Barnabas, who is often said to 'encourage' others. When Timothy is told to give himself to 'the encouragement', it seems — as we have seen — to be describing exposition of the passages read as lections in the synagogue or church. The absence of any specific reference need not be taken as an indication that this gift was never given to women, any more than the absence of the word 'saint' in the feminine need mean that women could not be saints. We know that women prophesied and that was also said to result in people being 'encouraged' as well as 'learning'. In the Old Testament we certainly know that *Deborah* encouraged Barak (Judges 4:6-8).

Evangelists

This gift is only once mentioned, as we have seen (Eph 4:11), and Philip is referred to as 'the evangelist' (Acts 21:8) presumably to distinguish him from Philip the apostle. The rarity of the word, then, should make us cautious about attaching any significance to the fact that no woman is ever specifically named as being an evangelist, although the reference to all the disciples from Jerusalem scattered abroad and evangelising (Acts 8:1,4) must surely include some female disciples, unless we are to assume gratuitously what Scripture does not say, namely that only male disciples were scattered and went evangelising. Paul, after all, calls the two women in Philippi, Euodias and Syntyche (Phil 4:3), not only 'fellow workers' or 'colleagues' *(synergon)*, but also 'members of the same team' *(synathlountes)* together with Paul and Clement. This certainly suggests that women shared in evangelism and church planting.

Faith, Healing, and Miracles

There are no specific references to any women by name exercising these gifts, but then apart from the apostles Peter and John (Acts 3:1ff; 5:12); Stephen (Acts 6:8); Ananias (Acts 9:17) and Paul (Acts 9:11) there are no indications of ordinary rank and file men believers named as doing such signs and wonders either. Hebrews 11 mentions the faith of Rahab (v 31) and says that 'women received back their dead raised to life again' (v 35) which seems to suggest they exercised faith (in the context of the whole chapter) even if others may have raised their dead. In fact, nobody uses much energy arguing about these points, for it is more especially in relation to teaching and to leading that problems arise.

Gifts of Service

The list given by Paul (I Tim 5:10) of qualifications for widows, who are to be supported by the church is instructive: 'and is well-known for her good deeds, such as bringing up children, showing hospitality, washing the feet of the saints, helping those in trouble and devoting herself to all kinds of good deeds.' These would seem to correspond with the acts of mercy described in the Romans list of gifts as 'showing mercy' (12:8). In this case we do know, the name of one woman, *Tabitha* or Dorcas, 'who was always doing good and helping the poor' (Acts 9:36). In this area nobody has any problems about the ministry of women, but we must recognise that these also are *charismata* given by the Spirit.

Administration (Leadership)

Administrations is the gift named in the Corinthian lists that would seem to correspond with the Romans gift of 'one who leads' as discussed in the earlier section (see p 88). Men are described as being leaders (for example Judas Barsabbas and Silas, Acts 15:22), but women are never specifically so described. This is surely true. But several comments seem pertinent at this point.

Many plural words to describe groups of people could include both males and females, and with most of them we would have no problems. Thus it is generally accepted that such plurals as 'saints', 'disciples', 'believers', 'priests' and even 'brethren' include Christians of both sexes. The same goes for 'men' *(anthropoi)*, reckoned as meaning the human species in general rather than 'males' *(androi)* in particular. But with 'deacons' and 'elders' we get much more cautious. Fortunately the woman *Phoebe* of Cenchrea is specifically described as being a deacon *(diakonos)*. Tabitha *(Dorcas)* is the only person of whom the word 'disciple' is used in the feminine form *(mathetria* rather than *mathetes,* Acts 9:36), otherwise purists might have argued that according to Scripture no woman was ever called a disciple!

There is the further reference in I Tim 3:11 to 'In the same way, *the women* ... '. These women are sometimes taken to be deacons' wives, that is, 'their wives', but there is no possessive pronoun in the original, and it seems strange if that is what is intended that we have no corresponding section about the demeanor proper to bishops' wives! We know that they were normally married because of v 2 'husbands of one wife'. But more than this the marker *hosautos* 'likewise' is used first of the deacons (comparing them with bishops) and then of the women, inferring that the women are in some way a parallel class to the bishops and the deacons.

But if we know that a woman can be a deacon, why should she not also be an elder? Some would say that she cannot because it says that an elder is to be the husband of one wife (v 2), except that the same thing is said of deacons (v 12), and we know that a woman can be a deacon. So it seems to mean that if a man is married, he must be beyond reproach in sexual matters, that if he has children they must be decently behaved, but he may have no children, or no wife or not even be a man at all!

There are other words used which describe the involvement of women in Christian ministry. In Romans 16, apart from Phoebe, Priscilla, and the possible apostle Junia, four other women are described as 'labouring in the Lord': in v 6 '*Mary* who worked very hard for you' and in v 12 'Greet *Tryphena* and *Tryphosa*, those women who worked hard in the Lord. Greet my dear friend *Persis*, another woman who worked very hard in the Lord.'

The same verb *kopiao* is used by the apostle Paul in two other ways: of his own apostolic labours (I Cor 15:10; Col 1:29) and of the labours of elders (I Thess 5:12; I Tim 5:17). It seems a fair assumption that the same expression used of these women singled out in this chapter for especial commendation is equally a reference to Christian work, that is, ministry in a church context and not merely housework in a domestic role.

We have already noted that the second word used of Phoebe — *prostatis* — is a much stronger word than 'helper' or 'succourer' and ought better to be translated as 'patroness', and perhaps even 'leader' for it is a cognate of the word used elsewhere for 'leaders' *(prohistamenoi)*.

This examination of the Scriptures suggests that a much better case can be made for the ministry of women than is generally recognised. Paul commends the ministry of women in Romans 16, and the apostle must be consistent with himself (and more important, the Scriptures must be consistent with themselves), for he would scarcely condemn in one place what he commends in another.

Discernment, Tongues, and Interpretation

There seems no reason for suggesting that women should not be equally endowed with these gifts as their brothers, and this has not been the focus of any disagreement between Christians that I know of.

While no women in Scripture are specifically named as evidencing these gifts, the classic exposition of the gifts says, 'When you come together, *everyone* has a hymn, or word of instruction, a revelation, a tongue or an interpretation ... if *anyone* speaks in a tongue, two − or at the most three − should speak' (I Cor 14:26-27). At this point there seems to be no distinction made between the sexes, and it does not say 'every man' or 'any man'. Further, apart from the apostle Paul, no male is specifically named as exercising tongues or interpretation, either. More, the 120 who spoke in tongues on the day of Pentecost did certainly include women (Acts 1:14 with 2:4 − 'all of them').

We have seen examples of the gift of discernment being exercised by the apostles Peter and Paul. Elizabeth's response to Mary is certainly prophetic, but also seemed discerning (Luke 1:41-45). Anna the prophetess also seems to have discerned who the baby was (Luke 2:38). Mary seems also to have discerned that Jesus might intervene in some way (John 2:3-5). It also seems that Mary of Bethany discerned more than others when she took the ointment and anointed the feet of Jesus with it − for Jesus said that it was 'for the day of my burial' (John 12:7). Priscilla is mentioned before her husband in discerning that Apollos needed to be more fully instructed in Christian truth (Acts 18:26). Indeed, most men might admit that women are more sensitive and observant of the needs of others than they themselves often are; and while this may be a natural gift, in spiritual women it is often sanctified by the Holy Spirit.

Conclusion

It seems worthwhile to ask, then, whether women partake of God's grace equally with men, and experience the spectrum of grace in the same way as men. It is always difficult to know whether one's own thinking is truly biblical or has been partly conditioned by one's own cultural expectations, but it seems to me that there is a spectrum of human characteristics — physical strength, ability to command, leadership — and that while men and women have many characteristics in common, there are some characteristics which might be thought to be more masculine or more feminine. It is certainly not true that all men are strong, wise and masterful, and all women weak, clinging, and silly. In the Providence of God not all men are up one end of the spectrum and all women at the other end of the spectrum of human characteristics. Some gifted women would seem to have gifts of leadership, and may be eloquent politicians, lawyers, or television interviewers. The spectrum of spiritual gifts may perhaps relate also to humanness, so that one may be superimposed upon the other. It may be that the Lord in His sovereignty puts more men at one end of the spectrum, and fewer women, but we cannot limit his sovereignty, and he is free to give grace and gifts to whomsoever he pleases. We must be sure also that it is not male prejudice, chauvinism, or culturally conditioned conservatism that makes us slow or reluctant to give opportunity to women to exercise spiritual gifts in the churches. This chapter has endeavoured to show that the

Scriptures do seem to show women exercising many functions in the early churches, and that we have no warrant to
disqualify them from the use of those spiritual gifts which
they were seen to have exercised then.

More, women have often been the backbone of the local
church in spite of all the disabilities under which they have
laboured. And we confidently expect that those churches
which can fully mobilise their women will be those which
grow most rapidly. Even the most conservative groups will
recognise that it is appropriate at the very least for women
to train women. To make our sisters in Christ feel frus-
trated, disregarded, undervalued is to hurt those who are
one with us in the body, and to retard the progress of the
churches towards a perfected Church Universal.

Let us rather encourage women to exercise all those gifts
which the Lord in His sovereignty is pleased to bestow
upon them. Paul envisaged that the unmarried would be
free of distractions in order to 'serve the Lord' (I Cor 7:34).
Peter describes married women (and he seems to have
travelled with his wife according to I Cor 9:5) to their
husbands 'as heirs with you of the gracious gift of life' (I
Peter 3:7). We have the same responsibility to the women
in the congregation to help them develop their gifts, as we
have to the men, and perhaps especially to our own wives.

Footnotes

[1]Elaine Storkey, *What's Right with Feminism* (SPCK/Third
    Way Books: London, 1985), pp 6, 24ff.

[2]C E B Cranfield, 'Romans', *International Critical Commentary*
    (T & T Clark: Edinburgh, 1979), vol II, p 789.

[3]John Chrysotom, 'Interpretation of the Letter to the
    Romans', col 669ff, in J-P Migne, ed, *Patrologia Graeca*
    (LX), Paris, 1857-1866.

[4]Richard Baxter, *Christian Directory*, II, ch 1, p 17.

[5]Storkey, *op cit*, p 52.

[6]Wayne Meeks, *The First Urban Christians* (Yale, 1983), p 79ff.

CONCLUSION

What response can we make to this discussion? One cannot assume that every reader will agree with the author's understandings. Some of you will certainly disagree with some of my conclusions. All of us feel threatened when our own interpretations are questioned. At the least I hope that you will accept that some fellow Christians interpret some of the spiritual gifts in a rather different way, and for sound reasons. They believe the Word of God no less than we do, but they see that particular words used to describe individual spiritual gifts may be understood in at least two different ways. We may continue to feel that our definition is the better one, but at least we can allow that others are equally sincere in holding a different interpretation.

The purpose of the gifts is to edify the church, and on that we can all agree. It is tragic if we so magnify 'the gifts' that we divide and splinter the church in consequence. For the gifts are only a means to an end, not an end in themselves. In writing about spiritual gifts in I Corinthians 12 and 14, Paul — led by the Holy Spirit, the author of Scripture — makes exactly this point in I Corinthians 13. Gifts are a temporary means to a great eternal end. They will 'pass away', temporary means of grace, part of the seeing-in-a-glass-darkly, knowing-in-part, spiritual-kindergarten world that will one day be brought to an end when we see him face to face. Paul specifies tongues, prophecy, knowledge, faith to perform miracles, generosity, and martyrdom, in that order, as worth nothing without the fruit of the Spirit, specifically love (I Cor 13:1-3). He then specifies prophecies, tongues, and knowledge, in that order, as gifts that will cease and pass away. What matters is not the means, but the end. We shall not take gifts to heaven with us, but we shall take with us what 'remains': faith, hope and love. And love is the greatest because faith will be lost in sight, and hope will have been fulfilled. God is never called either hope or faith, but he is called love. Spiritual gifts, then, have more to do with perfecting the church until we all arrive at the 'unity of the faith', while the fruit of the Spirit is what we need in order to maintain the 'unity of the Spirit' (cf Eph 4:2).

Above all let us rejoice and revel in God's gifts. Even if we do differ in the way we understand a few of them, we do all believe that God pours his grace upon his church so that we may speak and act in ways which edify the church and glorify His name. Let us not take from each other that joyful experience of being used by the Lord the Spirit to be a blessing to one another, or indeed detract from the joy of the Giver of every good and perfect gift. The Lord is the one to whom we belong and whom we serve, and we rejoice in all the grace he pours upon us, so that we can all testify:

> *When I feel the touch*
> *Of your hand upon my life*
> *It causes me to sing a song*
> *that I love You, Lord.*[1]

Footnote

[1] K Jones and D Matthews, 'When I Feel the Touch', *Luis Palau, Mission to London Praise* (Kingsway: Eastbourne, 1984).

BIBLIOGRAPHY

Atkinson, David. *Prophecy*. Grove Booklets on Ministry and Worship, No 49, 1977.

Aune, David. *Prophecy in Early Christianity and the Ancient Mediterranean World*. Eerdmans: Grand Rapids, 1983.

Barratt, C K, *A Commentary on the First Epistle to the Corinthians*. Black: London, 1971.

Baxter, Richard. *Christian Directory*. Orme Edition *Works*.

Bittlinger, Arnold. *Gifts and Graces: Commentary on I Corinthians 12-14*. Hodder & Stoughton: London, 1967.

Bridge, Donald. *Signs and Wonders Today*. IVP: Leicester, 1985.

Bridge, Donald and David Phypers. *Spiritual Gifts and the Church*. IVP: Leicester, 1973.

Bruce, F F. '1 and 2 Corinthians'. *New Century Bible*. Oliphants: Basingstoke, 1971.

Caird, G B. *The Language and Imagery of the Bible*. Duckworth: London, 1980.

Clark, Stephen B. *Spiritual Gifts*. Dove: Pecos, New Mexico, 1969.

Cranfield, C E. B. 'Romans'. *International Critical Commentary*. T & T Clark: Edinburgh, 1979.

Craston, Colin, ed. *The Charismatic Movement in the Church of England*. CIO Publishing: London, 1981.

Dunn, James D G. *Jesus and the Spirit*. SCM Press: London, 1975.

Edwards, Jonathan. *Works*. London, 1840.

Ellis, Earle. 'The Role of the Christian Prophet in Acts', in Gasque and Martin. *Apostolic History and the Gospel*. Paternoster Press: Exeter, 1970.

England, Ann, ed. *We Believe in Healing*. Marshall Pickering: Basingstoke, 1982.

Frost, Henry W. *Miraculous Healing*. Marshall, Morgan and Scott: Basingstoke, 1951.

Glover, A E. *A Thousand Miles of Miracle in China*. Pickering & Inglis: Basingstoke, 1919.

Goldingay, John. *The Church and the Gifts of the Spirit*. Grove Booklets on Ministry and Worship, No 7, 1972.

Green, Michael. *I Believe in the Holy Spirit*. Hodder & Stoughton: London, 1975.

Griffiths, Michael. *Cinderella's Betrothal Gifts*. OMF Books: Sevenoaks, 1978.

Griffiths, Michael. *Three Men Filled with the Spirit*. OMF Books: Sevenoaks, 1969.

Grudem, Wayne. *The Gift of Prophecy in First Corinthians*. University Press of America: Maryland, 1982.

Hemphill, K S. *The Pauline Concept of Charisma*. Cambridge PhD Dissertation, 1976.

Kelly, J N D. *The Pastoral Epistles*. Black's New Testament Commentaries. Black: London, 1976.

Kittel, Gerhard. *Theological Dictionary of the New Testament*. Eerdmans: Grand Rapids, 1972.

Lewis, C S. *Miracles*. Centenary Press: London, 1949.

Meeks, Wayne. *The First Urban Christians*. Yale University Press: New Haven, 1983.

Morris, Leon. *I Corinthians. Tyndale New Testament Commentaries*. IVP: Leicester, 1958.

Morris, Leon. *Ministers of God*. IVP: Leicester, 1964.

New Bible Dictionary. IVP: Leicester, 1962.

Orr and Walther. 'I Corinthians'. *Anchor Bible*. Doubleday: New York, 1976.

Owen, John. *The Holy Spirit*. Sovereign Grace Publishers: Grand Rapids, 1971.

Owen, John. *The Works of John Owen*. Banner of Truth: London, 1966.

Packer, J I. *Keep in Step with the Spirit*. IVP: Leicester, 1984.

Packer, J I. 'Jonathan Edwards and the Theology of Revival' in *Increasing in the Knowledge of God*. Puritan & Reformed Studies Conference Papers: London, 1961.

Samarin, W J. *Tongues of Men and Angels*. Macmillan: London, 1972.

Storkey, Elaine. *What's Right with Feminism?* SPCK/Third Way Books, 1985.

Stott, J R W. *The Preacher's Portrait*. Tyndale Press: London, 1961.

Stott, J R W. *Baptism and Fullness*. IVP: Leicester, 1975.

Turner, Max. 'Spiritual Gifts Then and Now'. *Vox Evangelica* 15 (1985).

Watson, David. *One in the Spirit*. Hodder & Stoughton: London, 1973.